Bulletin 57
1947

THE
REDUCTION OF
INTERGROUP TENSIONS:

A Survey of Research on Problems of Ethnic, Racial, and Religious Group Relations

By

Robin M. Williams, Jr.

SOCIAL SCIENCE RESEARCH COUNCIL
230 PARK AVENUE . . . NEW YORK 17

THE
REDUCTION OF
INTERGROUP TENSIONS:

A Survey of Research on Problems of Ethnic, Racial, and Religious Group Relations

By

Robin M. Williams, Jr.

Prepared under the direction of the Committee on Techniques for Reducing Group Hostility

SOCIAL SCIENCE RESEARCH COUNCIL
230 PARK AVENUE . . . NEW YORK 17

166392

The Social Science Research Council was organized in 1923 and formally incorporated in 1924. Its members are chosen from seven associated professional societies in the social sciences and from related disciplines. It is the purpose of the Council to plan and promote research in the social fields.

ASSOCIATED ORGANIZATIONS

American Anthropological Association

American Economic Association

American Historical Association

American Political Science Association

American Psychological Association

American Sociological Society

American Statistical Association

Committee on Techniques for Reducing Group Hostility

FOREWORD

FEW students of human relations during the period following World War I have failed to point to the widespread emergence at that time of many groups characterized by a high degree of aggressiveness and intolerance. In Italy, the Fascisti; in Germany, the Nazis; in Russia, the Communists; and in the United States, the Ku Klux Klan, were typical of the movements which thrived on hostility, intolerance, and the absence of practical effective nonviolent means of dealing with conflict situations. These groups explicitly advocated methods of violence and suppression in dealing with the social conflicts of which they were symptomatic expressions. The League of Nations, which was established as a mechanism for dealing with international strife, proved inadequate in the face of intransigent nationalism, and the underlying conflicts finally led to another costly World War.

It is now only too obvious that we are again confronted by a world seething with tensions and open conflicts among all kinds of racial, cultural, economic and political groups. It seems perfectly clear that the rapid discovery and application of practical effective techniques for the control of intergroup tension and hostility is one of the crucial needs of our time. This is equally true for both intranational and international communities.

Societies which are oriented toward the achievement of democratic goals have a particularly vital stake in the discovery of effective techniques for resolving group conflicts and reducing group hostilities. Implicit in democratic theory and practice is the acceptance of the fact of conflicting interests and even the positive encouragement of the expression of divergent views, aims, and values. However, there is the equally important assumption that conflicts can be resolved or accommodated by nonviolent means and that intergroup hostilities can be kept below the point where the basic consensus of the society is threatened. The survival of a democratic nation, therefore, depends on the invention of techniques for resolving its internal group conflicts in such a way that the welfare and interests of all elements of the community are given adequate consideration in the community. Nor can democratic values and practices long survive in an international world made up of intransigent societies organized for violent struggle. It is vital, therefore, that practical techniques for the nonviolent integrative solution of conflicts in the world community be devised and put into practice if democratic societies are to continue.[1]

It is fair to say that the critical nature of this problem is becoming clearer to increasing segments of the American public. And it is this increasing awareness which probably accounts in large part for important differences in our present orientation and efforts and those which obtained in the decade following 1918. One important difference is the wider acceptance of the necessity for the United States to participate more actively in international affairs in the interest of maintaining peace. Another important difference is the vastly greater amounts of money, time, and energy which many people are investing in a variety of organized efforts to resolve group conflicts and reduce group hostilities in our own social system. The amount of this investment is not known but there can be no doubt that the author of the present memorandum is safe in saying that there are hundreds of private and governmental agencies employing thousands of persons and spending millions of dollars in a sincere effort to do something about the problem.

This impressive development of action programs and agencies presents social scientists with an unprecedented opportunity and challenge. Without in the least detracting from the commendation that every citizen of good will has for the constructive actions of the agencies, it needs to be said that much of their work has involved a minimum of examination of basic assumptions and of testing the effects of the methods and techniques they employ. It is quite likely that many of the assumptions upon which actions and programs are based may be without very solid foundations; and more, that many of the methods and techniques employed may yield neutral if not negative results. There is every reason to expect that systematic analysis and experimentation in this field will contribute greatly to the increased effectiveness of practical action. What is more, such research should also yield rich returns in basic knowledge in the field of human relations.

In recognition of these opportunities and needs for research the Social Science Research Council established in September 1945 a Committee on Techniques for Reducing Group Hostility. The committee set as its first objectives the following:

---

[1] These remarks do not imply that force necessarily can be or should be eliminated from the technology of managing human affairs. But it is one thing to regard force as one of a number of techniques for resolving conflicts and one which is considered a last resort and at best a temporary means for dealing with a crisis; it is quite a different thing to regard it as the only or most important method for settling differences.

1. To make a preliminary survey of those techniques and procedures being used by various action agencies concerned with reducing tensions and conflicts among racial, cultural, and class groups in the United States

2. To propose research aimed at evaluating the effectiveness of these techniques and procedures

3. To consider social psychological theory and research bearing on the problem of group conflict with a view to deriving from any promising theory not now practically applied an action technique which might be tested for its effectiveness in reducing hostility and resolving conflict.

The present report prepared by Robin M. Williams, Jr., of Cornell University, is focused on the relations among racial, ethnic, and religious groups in the United States. In this report the author examines the more important techniques and procedures in use by representative action agencies which are seeking to reduce hostility and resolve conflict in interracial and intercultural group relations. He then analyzes the basic assumptions underlying the action programs and proposes research designed to test these assumptions. In connection with these proposals research which has relevance for these problems is discussed with a view to pointing out important gaps in our knowledge.

A particularly valuable section of the report is devoted to a presentation of major theorems and working hypotheses which bear on the problem of social conflict and which pose significant research problems.

Finally a representative series of desirable research projects are proposed and some illustrative project designs are outlined as suggestions for research planning.

Professional research workers will also find useful an appendix which includes a discussion of research methods and techniques applicable to the problems under consideration. The appendix also includes a well selected bibliography.

It is hoped that this research memorandum will prove a very useful aid and stimulus to social scientists working with public and private action agencies as well as those in academic and independent research institutions who are interested in contributing to more effective efforts in solving the problems of group tension and conflict in our society.

The committee and the author wish to express their appreciation of the help which many people have contributed to the completion of this report. Special mention should be made of the interest and cooperation on the part of the officials of many organizations whose work was reviewed by Dr. Williams. We wish also to thank The Rockefeller Foundation for its grant to the Social Science Research Council to make this study possible.

Committee on Techniques for Reducing Group Hostility

CHARLES DOLLARD
CARL I. HOVLAND
LEONARD S. COTTRELL, JR., *Chairman*

CONTENTS

CHAPTER I

INTRODUCTION

Purposes of This Report

The immediate objectives of this memorandum are to examine research needs and opportunities involved in the problem of reducing tensions among ethnic, racial, and religious groups, especially in the United States; to raise a limited number of questions which warrant intensified research effort; and to suggest some possibilities for fruitful testing of the more important hypotheses. In implementing these purposes the problem of intergroup hostility and the current approaches to ameliorative action will be surveyed briefly, and available research evidence as to the effects of control programs will be appraised. An attempt will then be made to set up a list of pertinent assumptions, principles, and working hypotheses concerning hostility, conflict, and techniques of control. Finally, possible research approaches and specific types of studies which seem to deserve concentrated attention in the immediate future will be presented.

Group Hostility as a "Problem"

Few things are more obvious in present day society than the great prevalence and intensity of hostility and conflict among various types of social groups. On the one hand, within a period of less than forty years there have been two world wars, a number of major revolutions, and dozens of undeclared wars, insurrections, rebellions, coups d'état, and other disorders of a mass-political character. On the other side, during this comparatively short period of recent history there has occurred an enormous proliferation of race riots, anti-Semitic disturbances, strikes and other labor-management conflicts, ethnic group clashes, and many disruptive movements based on systematic philosophies of hate and violence. Nazi systematization of "racialism," for example, posed a threat to fundamental democratic tenets and liberal institutions. Hardly anywhere in the major societies of the world could one find today a person who has not been touched by the crosscurrents of intergroup antagonism and conflict. These extraordinary demonstrations of human capacities for conflict could scarcely have failed to attract the attention of social scientists, statesmen, religious leaders, industrial and labor leaders, and many other responsible persons in the role of private citizens.

Hostilities and conflicts among intranational groups have evoked serious thought in recent years. When such hostility has taken the form of ethnic, religious, or racial cleavages it has had a particularly sharp impact because of its incompatibility with some of the most important historical values and cultural axioms of Western society. The incongruities are very clear in the United States. In the value-system which has been at least nominally dominant throughout most of American national history, a central element has been what may be called a "universal" ethic. This ethic formally enjoins certain important rules of behavior which are supposed to apply to everyone regardless of his particular status or group membership. At its most explicit level this type of principle appears in the Golden Rule, in the categorical value placed on honesty and fair play, in Constitutional and other legal requirements which stress rights and duties regardless of color, creed, class, or national origin. It is manifest likewise in the belief that individuals should be rewarded according to their personal qualities and achievements, rather than on the basis of birth in a particular group or class. Its ramifications can be traced in such seemingly unrelated things as competitive examinations for civil service positions, the one-price system, the code of being a good loser in competitive activities, the disapproval of nepotism and favoritism in public office, and a great variety of other beliefs and practices which are generally taken for granted. Discrimination and hostility among intranational groups identified on the basis of race, national origin, or religion thus come into conflict with a central theme of what Myrdal has called the American Creed.[1]

The marked development of sentiments of nationalism in the modern world has likewise sharpened awareness of internal conflict as a problem. In World War II recognition of the need for national unity in a warring world and of the threat of "divide and conquer" techniques called forth strong emphasis upon common American values and destinies. But the unifying sentiment that "we are all Americans" has often met qualifying and divisive definitions when applied to particular subgroups and classes: Negroes, Mexican or Spanish Americans, Jews, Catholics, Japanese Americans and many others.

Aside from their importance in such considerations of unity, intergroup relations within the United States have possible repercussions in international relations. In connection with such world events and issues as colonial problems, the great ferment in India, the "Asiatic solidarity" propagandized by the Japanese, the widely publicized policies of the Soviet Union toward minorities, and the question of Palestine, the role

[1] Gunnar Myrdal, *An American Dilemma* (New York: Harper & Brothers, 1944).

of the United States in the international scene may be profoundly affected by developments in the relations of domestic groups. American statesmen who deal with world problems have to contend with world-wide press coverage of intergroup relations in the United States.

On another level intergroup hostility has aroused concern because of its challenge to a pervasive strain of optimism, belief in progress, and faith in the perfectibility of human society which have deep roots in American culture. Belief in progress is an unstated assumption which underlies a common tendency of Americans to face social ills as problems and to say, "Let's do something about it." Serious problems of internal conflict are a fundamental challenge to this optimistic and activistic orientation.

Current problems of intergroup relations are further thrown into sharp relief by their existence against the background of a long period of great technological advance and rising levels of material welfare. Even with the cohesive pressure of war, there are such outbreaks as race riots in the most highly developed industrial and economic centers. Such contrasts raise questions as to the possibilities of understanding and control in the area of intergroup relations. The immediate postwar period accents this uncertainty; for wartime solidarity is always subject to strains as the external pressures are relaxed, the external outlets for aggression are reduced, and the sharing in a dramatic common effort is succeeded in some measure by the resurgence of separate interests and divisive claims.

All these facets of intergroup tensions are colored by their distinctive American context, a central aspect of which is the extraordinary heterogeneity of the people. All Americans, save the American Indians, are recent immigrants—as Will Rogers aptly pointed out with reference to the *Mayflower* tradition when he said that his ancestors "met the boat." The varied cultures from which our population stocks have come have made intergroup tolerance, at least, not just a virtue but in some senses a societal necessity. Insofar as the melting pot is a mythical concept—and certainly there is far from complete assimilation of all groups into a homogeneous way of life—some basis for intergroup tolerance and collaboration has been essential for the nation's existence as a social system. So long as each year brought large numbers of new immigrants, a shifting and flexible hierachy could develop in which each new group entered at the bottom of the "pecking order" only to move up later to a position of dominance over newer groups.[2] The diffuse character and

[2] This sort of progression in status was well illustrated by Irish immigrants to the United States. It obviously did not characterize Negro Americans.

shifting foci of many of the intergroup tensions which developed in this situation greatly mitigated their seriousness. In some respects also tensions were eased by an open economy with an expanding industrial system and large unexploited natural resources.

As a result of the cessation of large-scale immigration the racial, ethnic, and religious composition of the population is now becoming relatively stabilized. In the case of many population elements a gradual process of assimilation is blurring and erasing group differences. But certain other groups remain distinctive, either because of physical traits or because cultural traits of high visibility have been retained. Meanwhile, the national economy and social organization are beginning to exhibit traits of "maturity" and rigidity. In this situation intergroup tensions stand out with particular sharpness and, partly because of this, the impression that wholly new problems are emerging tends to develop.

The recognition of group conflicts in recent years has thus led to a sense of crisis which must be evaluated against historical perspective. There is a strong tendency in American thought to ignore or minimize the very considerable amount of intranational group conflict which has appeared in various periods of our history. Yet an examination of the record will show that internal hostilities and disorders have been by no means infrequent.[3]

There were many instances of organized violence in the early periods of "political" disorder, e.g., Bacon's Rebellion in 1667, the Revolution, and the series of insurrections in the early days of the Republic. Numerous slave revolts occurred before the Civil War. Anti-foreign and anti-Catholic agitation was more or less endemic for long periods, finding such expressions as the Know-Nothing movement of the middle nineteenth century. By the 1870's industrial strife had become important, exploding in the "Great Riots" of 1877 and again in the Pullman strike of 1894. Strikes with violence have appeared year after year. The long history of lynchings is well known. There have been three periods of race riots: in the first decade of the 1900's, immediately after World War I, and during World War II.

---

[3] Representative sources include: Bennett M. Rich, *The Presidents and Civil Disorder* (Washington: The Brookings Institution, 1941); A. F. Raper, *The Tragedy of Lynching* (Chapel Hill: University of North Carolina Press, 1933); Chicago Commission on Race Relations, *The Negro in Chicago* (University of Chicago Press, 1922); J. G. Miller, *The Black Patch War* (Chapel Hill: University of North Carolina Press, 1936); Arthur M. Mowrey, *The Dorr War* (Providence: Preston and Rounds Co., 1901); Leland D. Baldwin, *Whiskey Rebels* (Pittsburgh: University of Pittsburgh Press, 1939); Gustavus Myers, *History of Bigotry in the United States* (New York: Random House, 1943); Harvey Wish, "American Slave Insurrections before 1861," *Journal of Negro History*, 22:299–320 (1937).

Such sporadic outbreaks of open violence may be regarded as the more obvious "fevers" symptomatic of deeper, more widespread, and persistent hostilities and conflicts. The increasingly penetrating scientific analyses of the last few decades have made a substantial beginning toward discovery and description of the chronic situational factors linked to these continuing hostility patterns. In addition, there is increased understanding of the role of temporary changes conducive to intergroup tension. It is known that there is a minimum of group conflict, however difficult to specify, which arises from relatively permanent features of our society, such as the type of economic system, certain patterns of child training, and the way in which our distinctive family system is related to the competitive occupational structure. Further, this structural conflict is sometimes greatly exacerbated by social changes and temporary strains which are, so to speak, superimposed upon the more permanent sources of tension. World War II and its aftermath represent one such period of rapid change and correlative strain and tension. It is understandable that certain types of intergroup conflict might become conspicuous in this situation. Awareness of the seriousness and urgency of its problems is not incompatible with recognition that the problems are old, in kind if not in quantity, and that research and other action may well be focused on the continuing as well as the temporary features of the situation.

In this connection the title of the present memorandum requires some comment. Concentration of attention upon means for "reducing group hostility" may seem to rest upon an implicit value-premise: that the reduction of hostility is in itself a desirable goal regardless of other considerations. To take such an unqualified position in a publication of this nature would be both unnecessary and naïve. The only necessary assumption is that under *some* circumstances certain individuals and groups find it desirable to attempt to reduce hostility or conflict or both. Insofar as this is true, there is a social raison d'être for scientific study directed toward testing the results of various means used in these attempts. On the other hand, any mature research orientation in this field will explicitly recognize the possibility that from the standpoint of certain principles and values, a measure of intergroup hostility and conflict may sometimes be unavoidable, if not on occasion actually a means to the attainment of highly valued purposes. It is certain that instances can be pointed out, as for example in Negro-white relations, in which temporary intensification of conflict has led to changes which are widely regarded as improvements in terms of major values of American society. At the same time it can scarcely be doubted that much intergroup hostility is extremely costly, often in terms of standards accepted by all or most of the parties involved. There is at least a possibility that adequate solutions can sometimes be achieved at less social cost through avenues other than conflict. The extent to which techniques can be developed and utilized to reach such solutions will have much to do with the whole future of American—and world—society.

In brief outline, then, this is the context within which it is proposed to examine research needs and opportunities and to appraise the potential contributions of systematic study in the field of present interest. Chapter II begins this examination with a survey of present efforts to control intergroup relations and a summary of certain available research evidence as to the effects of such efforts.

CHAPTER II

APPRAISAL OF PROGRAMS IN INTERGROUP RELATIONS

Attempts To Reduce or Control Intergroup Hostility and Conflict

Recent years have brought a striking increase in the number and activity of organizations working in the field of intergroup relations. Problems growing out of war conditions gave impetus to the formation of such organizations, and the Detroit riot itself stimulated a wave of new agencies. As of 1945, there were 123 *national* organizations listed in an authoritative directory of agencies in race relations.[1] Of these, 75 were working "on a national basis to deal specifically with problems of intergroup relations. Even this list excludes Federal agencies, although some of these are among the most important in the field." [2] Regional, state, and local organizations undoubtedly run into hundreds. When to all these are added the many other groups and agencies which deal with or affect intergroup relations without having this as their central or explicit purpose, the multiplicity of efforts to "do something about" the problems sensed is a most impressive aspect of the current scene. Millions of dollars are being expended annually in direct attempts to influence intergroup relations, while thousands of people give their energy and talent to the work of organizations in this field. The amount of activity is eloquent testimony to both the recognized urgency of the problems and the amount of good will and civic concern which can be mobilized for action.

Existing organizations exhibit a wide variety of philosophies, aims, strategies, and technics. Johnson's classification of national agencies in race relations gives a good indication of the range:

A classification of the 75 organizations on the basis of strategies and techniques gives the following result: 15 agencies engage to some extent in programs of action and community organization; 13 are concerned with education in the schools; 37 carry on some form of adult education program; 10 promote cultural and recreational activities; 5 act through the courts to secure legal redress; 11 engage in serious research; and 7 are active primarily in promoting legislation. These are by no means mutually exclusive functions; actually, an organization may have several functions.[3]

---

[1] *Directory of Agencies in Race Relations* (Chicago: Julius Rosenwald Fund, 1945).
[2] Charles S. Johnson, "National Organizations in the Field of Race Relations," *The Annals*, 244:117 (1946).
[3] *Ibid.*, p. 118.

Under each of these broad classes of action are included many specific techniques which will be outlined subsequently.[4]

It is clear that organized attempts to improve intergroup relations are numerous and significant. Considering the seriousness of the problems, the possibly dangerous results of inappropriate action, and the very great amount of time and money involved, it might be anticipated that these agencies of social engineering would systematically check the effectiveness of their efforts by appropriate research. With only a few exceptions, however, this has not been done until very recently. Such agencies as the Commission on Community Interrelations have begun to operate on the principle, "no action without research, no research without action." Over most of the field it remains true, however, that the administrator, student, or interested citizen who wishes to gauge the comparative effectiveness of given programs or techniques can find little scientific evidence to guide him. Informed opinions based on practical experience and study can be had in abundance, and these are often invaluable. But established data and rigorous demonstration are almost nonexistent. Action programs sometimes involve surveys but such fact-finding efforts ordinarily result in static descriptions which afford little insight into causes and effects.

This dearth of appropriate research and consequent lack of a proven base for action is one of the most conspicuous features of existing intergroup programs.[5] The fact that educational and propaganda efforts constitute such a large proportion of the current activities makes the scarcity of research all the more striking since it is precisely among such groups as educators that greatest awareness of research needs and possibilities might be expected.[6] Whatever the reasons for this situation, it may be expected to change in the future, for among persons who are actively concerned with intergroup problems there is a rapidly growing recognition that an expanded program of rigorous research is urgently called for. To experienced practitioners much well intentioned activity seems wasteful and superficial, if not at times actually harmful. Enthusiastic efforts are sometimes launched on a large scale, unsupported by dependable evidence, and with no provision for testing of effects. In other

---

[4] See pp. 17–25, *infra.*

[5] Cf. the valuable survey by Goodwin Watson, "The Problem of Evaluation," *The Annals,* 244:177–182 (1946).

[6] "Evaluation efforts are almost nonexistent. There are no systematized measurements of changes of attitudes or intercultural growth in any one of these [public school] systems or communities, despite the fact that in at least one some program has been under way for about ten years." (Theodore Brameld and Eleanor Fish, "School Administration and Intercultural Relations," *ibid.,* pp. 31–32)

cases even the rule-of-thumb procedures which have been developed from long experience still lack validation. No matter how often a technique of action is used, it can yield no permanent increment to working knowledge unless results are rigorously checked in controlled situations.

The possibilities of important contributions to science from cumulative testing and controlled observation of programs for improving intergroup relations are sufficiently obvious. From another point of view the potential gains in terms of social policy and action are at least equally significant. New research tools, fresh theoretical insights, and the growing realism evident in social science approaches hold a promise which could hardly have been visualized a few decades ago. These developments should become a more usual and integral part of action programs for simple but fundamental reasons. Harmful attitudes result from the combination of several current factors: (1) there is an increased sense of the urgency of intergroup problems; (2) much purposive activity is aimed at the "improvement" of intergroup relations; (3) ameliorative efforts often encounter strong resistance, and sometimes eventuate in unexpected and undesired results. In many instances these circumstances lay the basis for a sense of disappointment, frustration, and helplessness which may easily turn into a philosophy of futility and fatalism. When well intentioned trial-and-error methods seem to fail or to produce only slow and halting progress, it is understandable that many people would conclude that intergroup hostility and conflict are inevitable—that nothing really important can be done about them. Such defeatism might well be avoided by scientific appraisal of the situation.

An alternate reaction to the results of present action programs is the feeling that intergroup tensions are so deeply imbedded in the nature of our whole social system that only a major alteration of the system could bring adequate solutions. To this, again, the verdict of "not proven" is appropriate; and in some instances this "total" orientation toward the problem may block constructive action in the present. On the whole it appears that naïve optimism is becoming less and less a major handicap in the efforts being made to improve group relations in this country. Of greater import is the disillusionment which can come from frustrated efforts and from unchecked judgments as to the possibilities of control.

In these terms, the contributions of research to action go beyond what are ordinarily thought of as "technical" problems. Insofar as research can demonstrate the results of particular policies and activities, it may be predicted that its cumulative findings will have a significant supporting and stabilizing influence upon philosophies of action. From what is

known now, we can anticipate that further study will show fairly
definite limits to the possibilities of controlling intergroup hostility
through any given set of techniques, but that it will also indicate the
circumstances in which control is feasible. The end result for the orientation of action should be to develop realistic confidence and to stabilize
expectations in such a way as to reduce the dangers of unchecked
utopianism on the one hand and fatalistic disillusionment on the other.

Basic Assumptions Underlying Action Programs

Research on the control of intergroup tensions requires as a first step
an analysis of the underlying *goals* and *causal assumptions* upon which
action is predicated. Inspection of existing programs shows that such
assumptions are very frequently implicit and taken for granted, and
that it is sometimes problematic how much awareness exists as to the
implications of the actions which are in fact undertaken.[7] Often, perhaps
even typically, a single agency is aiming toward several goals at the same
time: It may be engaged in carrying on law suits, organizing intergroup
conferences, preparing and disseminating propaganda, bringing pressure
to bear on legislative bodies, and carrying on research. There are instances
in which some of the assumptions which may be inferred from the
programs in operation appear to be incompatible with the nominal
objectives of the organization. Thus it may happen that an organization
which states its goals in terms of increasing mutual understanding and
amity is carrying out a program against discrimination sufficiently
militant to increase conflict in the immediate situation, whatever its
long-term results.

Every action program must assume, above all else, that through organized purposive efforts it is possible to exert an appreciable degree of
control over intergroup behavior. Control is meaningful in terms of
specific groups in particular circumstances, but to speak of the possibilities of "society controlling its minority problems," for example, is mean-
ingless. What we can directly observe is the concrete behavior of
particular individuals, groups, or organizations. When we ask what
"we" can do about any social problem it is clear that "we" can not refer

---

[7] The appraisal made by Paul Baker a number of years ago still merits attention: "The
interracial organizations are not always conscious of the methods they use in making
adjustments. Frequently, the techniques which are obvious are not the ones most powerful
in shaping behavior." (*Negro-White Adjustment*, New York: Association Press, 1934, p. 11.)
However, the action-assumptions are being made increasingly explicit, e.g., the Bureau
of Intercultural Education has formulated a set of hypotheses upon which to base its
program, the Commission on Community Interrelations and the American Council on
Race Relations have done considerable self-analysis, and there are several other prominent
examples.

to an abstract total society but simply to particular parts of the society. There are definite possibilities and limitations as to the control which can be achieved by any given agency or group with a certain position in the social structure, with certain funds and personnel at its disposal, with particular authority or power, with defined channels of communication, and so on. Choices of alternative methods and techniques are likely to be profoundly affected by the kind of judgments made as to the degree of control possible.

Beyond this, existing programs differ in the goals which they assume are worth while or feasible. At one extreme are those activities which seem to be guided by the assumption that the final goal is complete acculturation of different ethnic or, more rarely, racial and religious groups to one relatively homogeneous set of beliefs and behavior patterns. This orientation is historically derived from the melting-pot theory with its emphasis on "Americanization" or assimilation. Although this extreme version is much less common now than in the past, it is still manifest in some current intercultural programs. The opposite assumption visualizes a mosaic type of society in which many separate groups retain their traditional cultural characteristics and in which there is a minimum of contact among different groups; for the integration of the whole society reliance is placed on philosophies of tolerance, supported by common and interlocking economic and political interests, or on various kinds of suppression and authoritative controls. The "equal but separate" *modus vivendi* which so often has been invoked in Negro-white relations derives in part from this basic postulate. Somewhere between these contrasting points of view, so far as cultural groups are concerned, is the orientation known as cultural pluralism or "cultural democracy." Although often a vague and somewhat inconsistent position, cultural pluralism as usually represented envisions an end-situation in which (1) a considerable portion of the cultural distinctiveness of various groups will be retained, but (2) there will be extensive interaction among all groups, and (3) at least a minimal body of *shared* values and traditions will be emphasized.

Recently there has been more and more serious questioning of both the possibility of actually eradicating differences in any near future and the value of such a goal, even if it could be achieved. To many, the melting pot has begun to represent flat uniformity imposed by a dominant group. The persistence of existing cultural differences has been increasingly recognized as bound up in many ways with fundamental sources of individual and group integrity. At the same time workers in the field of intergroup relations have seen the impressive growth of extensive intergroup contacts in an industrial, urban, secular, mobile society. Intergroup problems have become less sharply localized. Physical separation of groups has become more difficult to maintain. Aside from other factors, including that resistance to any form of "segregation" which the nominally dominant American value-system encourages, these facts in themselves have cast serious doubt upon even the feasibility of a mosaic-type society. Thus, in effect, doctrines of cultural pluralism have represented a compromise solution, conscious or unconscious, of the dilemmas just sketched.

Another important axis of decision involves questions as to the relative weight to be given to the achievement of gains in group status, rights, and privileges as against the avoidance of conflict and the preservation of harmonious intergroup relations. These questions entail complex considerations of pace and timing under varied circumstances. Existing agencies have made contrasting decisions, so that we have such comparisons as that between the Congress of Racial Equality and the National Association for the Advancement of Colored People, on the one hand, and the Southern Regional Council or the Urban League, on the other. The labels of "militancy" or "gradualism" often more nearly reflect contrasting choices of pace than differences in ultimate purposes.

The choice of major goals and strategies, whether wholly deliberate or partly unwitting, is a recurrent problem of all agencies in the field of intergroup relations. Discussions of the differential consequences have been continuous over a long period. With respect to fundamental value-premises, discussion always reaches the point at which factual questions are exhausted and there remains only argument over ultimate purposes. There is still, however, an important need for careful analysis, necessarily on a comparative historical basis, of the actual concomitants or consequences of action based on the different value-assumptions possible in past situations. Some analysis of this kind has been made, but more thorough and systematic study may help to resolve some of the questions upon which opinion is still divided.

Action requires not only a choice of goals but also a selection of means—a selection which is affected by the ends chosen but not completely determined by them. The selection of means also rests upon cause-and-effect assumptions: if *this* is done, then *that* will follow. Analysis of the specific causal assumptions which are implied in current action programs amounts to a formulation of a great many particular hypotheses. Since a number of possible hypotheses are presented in Chapter III, here it is necessary only to outline a few of the broadest premises which appear to operate in the selection of methods and techniques in actual programs.

1. One of the most obvious of these premises guiding strategy is, in its least sophisticated formulation, "Give people the facts and prejudice will disappear." In this crude form the assumption is rarely made explicit, yet much intercultural activity is carried on as if the proposition were accepted. A recent critique of educational programs maintains: "Perhaps the most glaring defect of intercultural education as it functions at present is that it is geared for the most part only to intellectual values. It assumes—an assumption yet to be empirically confirmed—that ignorance is the real barrier, that the truth will set men free, that the objective facts about race and race prejudice are sufficient automatically to eliminate bias and suspicion and hatred." [8] Under repeated criticisms of this sort, the claims made for the imparting of information are growing more modest, frequently taking the form of asserting no more than that "the facts will have *some* influence." Even this is sometimes qualified by indicating the need for a relatively long period and many cumulative and mutually supporting educational influences.

Insofar as it is assumed that presentation of facts will reduce intergroup prejudice, a further premise is necessary: that prejudice is unrealistic, a function of ignorance or of "distorted stereotypes," of "false pictures in the mind," of "warped social perception." For unless prejudices represent erroneous information or ignorance, the presentation of correct facts can not be expected to change the hostile attitudes.[9] An implicit belief in the efficacy of information is extremely common [10] and is often expelled in one context only to reappear in another.

In one sense the opposite of the viewpoint just mentioned is the doctrine that group prejudices are subject to reduction or elimination *only* by changing "underlying interests" or "needs." This assumption most commonly takes the form of stressing, and acting on the basis of, a belief in the dominant importance of economic competition and

[8] Charles I. Glicksberg, "Intercultural Education: Utopia or Reality," *Common Ground,* 6(4):64(1946).

[9] It does not necessarily follow, of course, that presentation of facts would be the only way to change even a prejudice which was a function of inadequate or false information.

[10] Even where there is a careful recognition of the multiple origins of prejudice, isolated statements may imply that the central element is a false stereotype which may be brought into line with the facts, which are assumed to differ from the stereotype. Thus: "The practical goal of studying prejudices is to provide a foundation for changing prejudices so as to square the stereotypes with the facts." (Ronald Lippitt and Marian Radke, "New Trends in the Investigation of Prejudice," *The Annals,* 244:176)

economic deprivation. This often underlies the efforts of those who attack intergroup problems by working for measures intended to provide greater economic security for all, to increase job opportunities for "underprivileged" elements, and so on. An extreme development of the postulate that economic interests are determinants of prejudice leads to diagnosis in terms of alleged inevitable consequences of a competitive, capitalistic system; the corollary program of action is then sometimes visualized as a fundamental transformation of at least some aspects of the economic and political structure. Thus it is said that prejudice is not a "moral problem" but represents an ideology maintained because of its usefulness in perpetuating a system of differential privileges. In this view prejudice can be eradicated only by altering the social structure which gives rise to "interests" that are served by intergroup hostility along the lines of racial, ethnic, or religious groupings.[11]

On the other hand, among those who stress certain psychological needs as the central element in prejudice, there is sometimes a tendency to assume that direct change in the individual's emotional organization is the major effective strategy which can be employed. This psychiatric emphasis, however, has met with weighty objections when presented as an exclusive approach, e.g., limitations of time and trained personnel, the pervasive influence of group situational factors, and the consequent frequency of "relapses." At present it is not a common assumption among agencies working in the area of intergroup relations. The question of how much emphasis should be placed upon treatment of individuals' emotional needs, however, does suggest the more general question to be outlined next.

2. A second basic assumption underlying a great variety of specific techniques may be presented in two opposing formulations: that action should be directed toward (a) a direct change in values or attitudes, *or* (b) a change in those aspects of the situation which are regarded as productive of existing attitudes and behavior. Very few concrete programs are based exclusively on one or the other. With the rather elaborate specialization of agencies which has come about, part of the varying emphasis toward one pole or the other represents a kind of division of labor and not necessarily an unconditional espousal of one as the only approach. Furthermore, many groups which confine their activity largely to education and publicity are well aware of the importance of situational

---

[11] An almost pure example of this approach is found in Herbert Aptheker's *The Negro People in America* (New York: International Publishers, 1946).

factors. But they often find these factors inaccessible to control under existing circumstances and so concentrate upon direct influencing of attitudes.[12] Although the choice of approaches is thus not a clear index of cause-and-effect assumptions, it is true that such opposing assumptions are made, corresponding activities are carried out in many specific situations, and definite opinions are held as to the feasibility, effects, and costs of the alternative programs. But again, the systematic evidence which would be required to reach a scientific judgment on the merits and demerits of these alternatives for meeting a range of social situations does not yet exist.

3. "Contact brings friendliness." This is the extreme and unqualified phrasing of a general assumption manifest in a great many current activities.[13] Some of the more specific hypotheses which can be derived from available research and other experience bearing on this assumption are outlined in Chapter III. At this point we need only note that there is evidence that some kinds of contact sometimes are followed by increased mutual understanding and friendliness, and that the reverse is also true. There is a growing awareness that future action and research must define the whole context of intergroup contacts more carefully in order to arrive at practically useful specifications.

4. To what extent is it wise to focus public attention upon intergroup relations, upon the problems they represent, and upon changes or attempts to bring about changes in group relations? What are the effects of publicizing intergroup tensions and instances of hostile behavior? Should the *intergroup* character of contacts be stressed or minimized? How should hostile rumors be handled? On questions of this kind the opinions of educators and administrators range from the belief that "the best way to handle intergroup relations is to say as little as possible about them" to the policy of singling out minorities and intergroup tensions for explicit attention.[14] In its most general form the issue is that of the differential consequences of direct and publicly labeled approaches as against indirect, nonmanifest methods of influencing group relations. In actual practice the policies range from continual emphasis on inter-

[12] In some cases the demands of the more militant groups for "action" rather than "words" reflect a feeling on their part that many information-education-propaganda efforts are largely "ritualistic" in the sense of having little effect and of serving as a substitute for efforts to change the real situation.

[13] The related but not completely homologous proposition is that segregation increases the likelihood of intergroup tension and hostility.

[14] Cf. Theodore Brameld, *Minority Problems in the Public Schools* (New York: Harper & Brothers, 1946), pp. 11, 14, 30, 161.

group labels to minimizing intergroup differences, avoiding the posing of direct issues-in-principle, relying on fait accompli techniques, and in general keeping intergroup problems from the center of attention.

Probably no other question of approach in this field has been more extensively—and heatedly—discussed than this. For all its vigor, the discussion has failed to produce definite conclusions or even an appreciable consensus of opinion. The only reasonably certain point is that no clear answer of "good" or "bad" can be expected when the question is raised in general terms; casual observation indicates that the results of alternative policies vary with the specific types of situations in which they are followed. What is needed first of all is a series of repetitive studies to determine the concomitants of particular actions, based upon assumptions at one pole or the other. Only when these studies are complete can we hope to arrive at verified general conclusions.[15]

5. The great amount of effort currently devoted to arranging special occasions for intergroup association would hardly be expended except for the assumptions that (a) the experience changes behavior, and (b) there is a transfer of the changed behavior to other, more usual, types of situations. Thus, an interracial summer camp is presumably not an end in itself, nor is such a project likely to be undertaken exclusively for the possible symbolic values for the public at large. Inferentially, it must be believed that the participating individuals will behave in appreciably more desirable ways in future situations. Analogies from transfer-of-learning studies concerned with skills and academic subjects are not very helpful in evaluating such a belief, for the social and emotional contexts are radically different. However, as far as can be discovered, there is now no scientifically acceptable evidence on behavior transfers from various types of special intergroup contacts to other situations.

The assumptions examined thus far do not include nearly all the orientations, nor even those of widest generality, implied by current activities. Enough have been described, however, to provide the background for a brief review of specific techniques which are employed in control programs. (Further consideration will be given to working assumptions and specific hypotheses in Chapter III.)

---

[15] It should go without saying that these statements do *not* imply (1) that action must wait until this terminal goal has been reached; nor that (2) even the most complete conceivable program of scientific study will settle all the practical problems of policy decision in concrete cases. In the first place, circumstances are indefinitely varied, and there is always need for seasoned judgment. Scientific analysis, however, can provide the data necessary for economy in decision making. Action, based on ordinary experience and reasoning, will continue; but it should have a progressively more dependable basis as research proceeds along these lines.

Techniques for Controlling Intergroup Relations

Fundamentally, there are only two avenues through which human behavior may be controlled.[16]

First, one may operate on *the situation within which people must act,* or upon their perception of the situation, without attempting directly to alter their attitudes, sentiments, or values. The pressure for a given type of behavior then comes either from (a) revealing information which affects the way in which individuals visualize the situation,[17] or from (b) actual or potential alteration of the situation itself. In the area of intergroup relations an example of the first type of pressure would be the effective imparting of facts convincing white workers that inclusion of Negro workers in an industrial union would increase the organization's bargaining power. A hitherto unrecognized aspect of the situation might thus become a factor in changed group relations. Random examples of the second type of alteration would include penalties for intergroup aggression, or rewards for cooperation; removal of legal disabilities; economic changes resulting in greater security and lessened competition in the occupational field.

Among organizations which are primarily and explicitly working on intergroup relations, the most common type of effort to change the actual situation is probably that of arranging for social contact between members of different groups. Such arrangements are of many different kinds, ranging from special, temporary and limited contacts to continuing and intensive association. Another approach designed to change a given situation is the establishment and maintenance of special-purpose organizations within a given group. This is exemplified by attempts to divert potentially disruptive activities of adolescents into constructive channels through boys' clubs and the like. It is illustrated also by more significant organizations for defense, protest, and pressure within minority groups. A third approach directed toward actual change in situational factors is through the law and law-enforcement; in the cases of Negroes, Japanese Americans, and certain immigrant groups, legal factors are the focus of much organized effort.

The second main avenue of control is through *direct appeal to the values or attitudes of individuals,* without necessarily changing the actual

[16] See Talcott Parsons, "Propaganda and Social Control," *Psychiatry,* 5:551–572 (1942). A somewhat different but compatible classification is given by Charles Strother, "Methods of Modifying Behavior," *Journal of Social Issues,* 1(3):46–52 (1945).

[17] Cf. the aphorism of W. I. Thomas: "If men define . . . situations as real, they are real in their consequences." ("The Relation of Research to the Social Process," in *Essays on Research in the Social Sciences,* Washington: The Brookings Institution, 1931, p. 189)

or potential situation of action in other respects.[18] Here belongs much of the whole panoply of propaganda: use of shared symbols, prestige appeals, redefinition of values, affirmation of moral norms, manipulation of anxiety and guilt, etc. Direct efforts to change attitudes on intergroup relations generally fall into a few fairly distinct types:

(1) The attempt is made by various specific techniques to show that differences in the characteristics of various groups are not inevitable or biologically fixed. This has been of first-rank importance in the case of the Negro.

(2) There is the approach which minimizes the differences in values and behavior, and stresses the elements common to both parties in the conflict. Thus, for example, important common elements in the religious beliefs and practices of Protestant, Catholic, and Jewish groups may be emphasized; or national membership and common socio-political beliefs may become the focus of attention.

(3) The range of intragroup variation is highlighted as a way of attacking categorical definitions of the situation. In this approach one assumption (explicit or implicit) is that the recognition of individual and subgroup differences will weaken stereotypes and introduce a realistic flexibility in intergroup attitudes.

(4) Appeal is made to larger social codes, religious values, or legal precepts. Approaches in this category are almost infinitely varied, including dramatization of Constitutional rights, and affirmation of codes of fair play and other ethical precepts. To be at all effective, efforts along these lines must be based upon an adequate consensus with regard to the relevant codes among the persons to whom the "propaganda" is directed. What constitutes an adequate consensus in any particular case is often a difficult problem of fact finding.

(5) Emphasis is placed upon those achievements and qualities of members of a specific group which are rather universally esteemed and especially upon those which do not fit the group stereotype. In the case of Negroes, for example, this may involve publicity concerning achievements in literature, science, medicine, military activity, business, and other fields apart from traditional "Negro arts." Qualities of dependability, integrity, serious industry and the like may be highlighted as an antidote to stereotyped pictures of contrary qualities.

[18] "There are two methods available for meeting this problem [ethnic conflict]: first by altering the actual or potential situations in which people act; second, by appealing to the sentiments of individuals without necessarily altering the situations but by manipulating symbols, changing attitudes or influencing their 'definition of the situation.'" (Simon Marcson, "The Control of Ethnic Conflict," *Social Forces*, 24:162)

(6) The desired behavior (tolerance, cooperation, etc.) is linked with persons who are prestige symbols and the objects of mass identifications on other grounds. This approach may use any of the preceding types of appeal, but implements them by association with particular, valued personalities. So, for example, motion picture actors with whom large proportions of the population are assumed to have made identification are shown appealing for or demonstrating the behaviors which are the goal of the propaganda effort. Under some conditions this technique may result in the important by-product of weakening the presumption of group support for hostile intergroup actions. This becomes highly significant when prestige symbols are used to redefine permissive behaviors, as when persons who symbolize authority publicly act to reinforce desired attitudes or to discourage undesired behavior. Persons who represent the dicta of conscience, especially religious leaders and political officers, frequently serve this function: Pope Pius XI issues an encyclical condemning anti-Semitism; a minister speaks out against group hostility; the President establishes a Committee on Fair Employment Practice.

The more specific techniques which have been used by agencies concerned with promoting intergroup cooperation or with improving the status of a particular group include almost every conceivable mode of influencing human behavior. Goodwin Watson has classified these activities into seven patterns: exhortation, education, participation, revelation, negotiation, contention, and prevention.[19] Three of these are primarily in the area of direct attempts to change attitudes or values— exhorting to ideal patterns, educating, and revealing new facts. Social contact across group lines (participation) represents a situational alteration which is assumed to affect subsequent behavior. The remaining patterns include both situational alterations and direct approaches to attitudinal change.

Watson's ordering of approaches helps to clarify the main types of current intergroup programs. For the present purpose of specifying research possibilities, however, a somewhat more detailed classification will be employed. We are interested in specific concrete actions which can be directly observed. Although it is doubtless true that no two situations involving intergroup relations are exactly the same, certainly a number of fairly specific patterns of action are repeated frequently in essentially the same form. As in other fields of behavior, the number of

---

[19] In a survey for the Commission on Community Interrelations, published as *Action for Unity* (New York: Harper & Brothers, 1946). A summary may be found in the Commission's *Facts on Friction*, No. 9 (February 1946).

possible patterns of intergroup activity is by no means unlimited. And
when we turn to observation of activities under way, the identification
and description of specific techniques becomes a manageable task.

The following list of methods currently used in purposive efforts to
affect intergroup relations is by no means exhaustive. For one thing,
it is heavily weighted with the more obvious and direct techniques; for
another, it is limited to recurrent and widespread patterns of action and
so does not show the indefinite variety of detail in techniques. It largely
omits certain crucially important indirect approaches such as educational
policy, economic developments or "reforms," and many public measures
which affect the general tension-level of the society.[20] However, the
classes of methods included are perhaps sufficiently numerous and important in their own right to suggest the great wealth of research needs
and opportunities which the field of intergroup action offers. Techniques
of action might be classified according to content or means. Thus consideration of propaganda on the basis of content would lead to classification in terms of specific themes or of general psychological characteristics (prestige-suggestion, generality, fear-appeal, etc.). Classification
according to means would be in terms of types of publication media and
so on. For our purposes it will be most convenient to list concrete means,
ignoring various analytical distinctions which could be made in each
case. On this basis, the following are the more important types of action
observable in current programs:

1. *Information, education, propaganda* [21]
   a. Preparation and distribution of pamphlets, brochures, leaflets, news-
      letters, comic books, posters, and similar materials
   b. Preparation and distribution of magazines, journals, books, news
      articles
   c. Radio broadcasting: providing scripts and speakers, arranging forums,
      dramas, etc.
   d. Preparation and distribution of motion pictures
      (1) Special films
      (2) Influencing usual commercial productions: news reels, short sub-
          jects and cartoons, regular commercial films

---

[20] Including fundamental structural changes in the economic and political fields.

[21] There is no necessity to enter into the usually sterile discussion of a distinction between
"education" and "propaganda." There are several bases of distinction which are useful
for certain purposes, but none which is especially relevant here. (Probably the clearest line
of demarcation in principle is that which divides the imparting of scientifically verified
facts from appeals to social norms and to values not subject to scientific validation. Of
course, in actual practice even this distinction is usually difficult to establish.)

e. Providing speakers for organized groups: labor unions, churches, schools and colleges, business and civic clubs, women's clubs, discussion groups, fraternal orders, etc.

f. Stimulating and arranging addresses by public leaders, especially government officials

g. Organizing certain types of mass meetings, e.g., the Los Angeles rally opposing a prominent anti-minority agitator

h. Stimulating, organizing, and furnishing materials for teacher training through usual educational channels

i. Providing workshops, seminars, and special courses for ministers, teachers, social workers, labor union workers, industrial managers and supervisors, municipal police, etc.

j. Influencing curricula, techniques, and materials in intergroup education in the public schools and other educational institutions

k. Action research in local communities. (See also No. 7 *infra*.)

Nearly all agencies concerned with intergroup relations use some of the techniques in this classification. In many instances their activities are almost exclusively in this category. Thus, the Institute for American Democracy concentrates entirely on advertising, weekly releases, and radio programs. The Common Council for American Unity devotes most of its effort to informational and educational tasks. The Bureau for Intercultural Education, as its name indicates, emphasizes especially patterns *h, i,* and *j.* The Public Affairs Committee is well known for its specialized work in producing significant pamphlets. The primary activity of the League for Fair Play is that of furnishing speakers to organized groups. The Commission on Community Interrelations of the American Jewish Congress publicizes results of action research. Over the entire field of group relations, the efforts which go into education and propaganda constitute a very high proportion of all current activities.[22]

2. *Political and legal pressures*

a. Local, state, and national "lobbies"

b. Law suits, test cases, injunctions and other court action; legal aid services

c. Specific mobilization of support for particular candidates, officials, parties, or programs

d. Organized demonstrations and protests, resolutions, telegrams and

---

[22] A recent analysis of thirty organizations working in the intercultural field "showed that by far the largest number confine their efforts to providing speakers, holding forum discussions, and publishing pamphlets." (H. H. Giles and William Van Til, "School and Community Projects," *The Annals,* 244:34)

letters, picketing, mass meetings and "marches" to influence legislation on policy, boycotts, and various kinds of "direct action" [23]

e. Investigation and exposure of illegal acts, or acts subject to public censure, committed by persons in anti-minority political movements

National organizations which emphasize some or all of these approaches include the American Civil Liberties Union, the National Association for the Advancement of Colored People, American Committee for Protection of Foreign Born, and the National Lawyers Guild, to mention only a few of the more important groups.

3. *Organization of intergroup contacts in industrial or other work situations*

a. Mixed work-groups in plant or shop
b. Mixed participation in union activities
c. Mixed staffs in educational organizations, hospitals, social service agencies, governmental agencies, etc.
d. Recreational and "social" activities growing out of occupational association

In this area the National Maritime Union of America has carried out a consistent policy of nondiscrimination. Several unions of the Congress for Industrial Organization likewise have worked actively to create intergroup solidarity. Some unions suspend members who refuse to work with other members of a different racial or ethnic group. Of group integration on the initiative of management probably the best known instance, although by no means the largest, is that of the National Smelting Company of Cleveland, Ohio. Mixed labor forces have been numerous during the war period, often without segregation.[24]

4. *Organization of intergroup contacts in nonvocational settings*

a. Special temporary interaction
   (1) Ceremonial exchanges, e.g., Race Relations Sundays, Brotherhood Weeks, etc.
   (2) Recreational activities: tours, camping trips, drama, music, etc.
   (3) Field trips to visit members of a different group
   (4) Arranged visits in the home
   (5) Joint participation in common secular or religious observances

[23] An interesting example of direct action of one type is found in the practice of members of the Congress of Racial Equality who, as an interracial group, seek service in restaurants or other commercial establishments where discrimination has been observed.

[24] See the survey by J. A. Thomas, "War-Time Changes in the Occupational Status of Negro Workers," *Occupations*, 23:402–405 (1945).

b. Continuing or repeated interaction
  (1) Any of the above insofar as they are recurrent
  (2) Young people's groups
    (a) YMCA and YWCA
    (b) Boy Scouts and Girl Scouts
    (c) Student organizations
    (d) Other educational, political, religious, or social organizations
  (3) Adult groups
    (a) Mixed membership in any group not explicitly devoted to intergroup relations
    (b) Intergroup conferences: arranging for consultation and discussion among group representatives
    (c) Intergroup forums on group relations
    (d) Intergroup councils and committees
    (e) Mixed residence groups in "Commons" of various kinds, in public housing projects, and in private residential areas

Attempts to establish personal associations between members of different groups are numerous and tremendously varied. The Department of Race Relations of the Federal Council of the Churches of Christ in America carries on an activity bordering this area in its promotion of the annual observance of Race Relations Sunday and Brotherhood Week—occasions which in some instances result in interracial contacts such as pulpit exchanges. Both Boy Scouts and Girl Scouts have conducted interracial camps. The YWCA has increasingly integrated minority members into local programs. In Vermont Rev. A. Ritchie Low has successfully arranged for children from Harlem to spend the summer with white parishioners who volunteered to take the children into their homes.[25] The number of established intergroup committees, forums, councils, etc. certainly runs into the hundreds. There are a number of interracial churches, and recent years have seen the establishment of housing projects with mixed constituencies in several cities.

Each of the various types of contact between members of different groups can be shown to be successful in some instances and unsuccessful in others. Careful analyses of the factors determining the different outcomes in particular cases have not yet appeared.

5. *Organization for adjusting intergroup differences:* activating channels for negotiation, conciliation, and mediation and for the use of

[25] A. Ritchie Low, "Invitation to Vermont," *Common Ground,* 6(4):44–52 (1946).

persuasion and other direct influences in dealing with particular groups and individuals

Frequently the channels for this pattern of activity are informal and not immediately obvious. Among the large formal organizations using these techniques as part of their total program are the National Urban League, the American Council on Race Relations, and the Southern Regional Council.

6. *Public commendations and awards* for individuals or organizations working for improved intergroup relations

The Department of Race Relations of the Federal Council of the Churches of Christ in America for years has given public commendation for certain achievements in interracial relations.[26] An annual award for "outstanding service in the field of race relations" is presented by a committee for the improvement of race relations of the Uptown Chamber of Commerce in New York City. There are a number of other examples.

7. *Psychotherapy with individuals or small groups*
    a. Psychodrama or sociodrama
    b. Clinical therapy
        (1) Individual } utilizing the many specific techniques of psychiatry
        (2) Group   } and clinical psychology

Under the influence of J. L. Moreno, a number of scattered attempts to use role-playing techniques as a means of changing intergroup attitudes are being undertaken. Carl Rogers has suggested that nondirective therapy may be effective in resolving prejudices and conflicts. Some of the "group training" work by such men as G. Bavalas and Ronald Lippitt is marginal to those techniques.

8. *Organization of activities of groups considered likely sources of conflict:* boys' clubs, recreational areas, etc.

Most of the examples of this technique are initiated under local sponsorship. In many instances the organizations are on an intergroup basis.

9. *Fact finding*
    a. Studies by technical specialists or by various types of "investigators"
        (1) Findings disseminated to the general public
        (2) Findings communicated only to particular individuals or groups
    b. Studies by nontechnicians

[26] G. E. Haynes, "Public Approbation as a Means of Changing Interracial Attitudes and Customs," *Social Forces*, 24:105–110 (1945).

    c. Studies with technical guidance, but participated in by individuals in
       a position to take action

This category overlaps the first, but represents a highly specialized
technique which warrants special listing.[27] It includes not only research
under academic auspices but also "action research" and certain activities
of organizations such as the Friends of Democracy and the Anti-
Defamation League. The interracial clinics sponsored by the Federal
Council of Churches also carry on group fact-finding activities.

Incomplete as it is, this list shows a rather bewildering variety of
approaches to the goal of reducing or channelizing intergroup tensions.
Yet, all the diverse techniques involve the central research problem of
determining the actual consequences of the various approaches. Recognition of this fact brings us directly to the issue: how can research establish
the effects of control programs in this field?

Nature of Evidence Required To Establish Effects of Control Measures

    Clearly this question involves the problem of attaining "adequate
proof," which is crucial in all scientific investigation. This is as obvious
as the fact that there are varying levels of proof, ranging from tenuous
indications to an approximation of rational certainty. As the rigor of
demonstration departs from the ideal standard of "certainty," what may
be considered adequate evidence in any one science or any one test
becomes increasingly problematic. For purposes of social action it is
frequently necessary to accept propositions with less proof than would
usually be required to meet scientific standards. Therefore, when it is
asked what evidence is required to determine the effects of attempts to
control intergroup relations, the answer can not be given in all-or-none
terms. There is no sharp fixed line between adequate and inadequate
evidence; the requirements vary with the scope and accuracy of prediction which is considered necessary in any particular instance. It is
possible, however, to specify the conditions of definitive proof, on the
one hand, and to outline certain minimum conditions which must be
met by any propositions for which more than common-sense status is
claimed, on the other.

Maximum adequacy of proof may be considered attained when these
conditions are met: (1) The operations of observation are objective, i.e.,
can be described, communicated, and duplicated by other trained ob-

---

[27] The necessary inclusion of fact finding among techniques of action suggests that
research must be seen as an integral part of intergroup relations. Scientific study is a form
of social action; the extension of research to intergroup action is not without social
significance in itself.

servers. (2) The variables are defined and recorded (measured, ranked, classified, or presence-absence noted). (3) One factor or set of factors (*x*) is shown to be present whenever an "effect" (*y*) is present, and *y* never appears without *x*, when all other relevant factors are held constant. (4) The relation of factors is meaningful in terms of a systematic theory. The linkage of *x* and *y*, under the specified conditions of constancy in other factors, may be established by purposive manipulation of the situation, or by finding "natural" situations, or by symbolic manipulation of variables. The presumed linkage can be tested by its predictive value—by introducing *x* with the prediction that *y* will appear under defined conditions.

Minimum adequacy of evidence for any generalization claiming scientific status as more than a hypothesis would seem to entail the first two conditions stated, plus some systematic evidence of a relation between the factors under consideration. A generalization, to differ from "personal opinion" or "common sense" must be objective—capable of repeated establishment by operations which can be communicated—and the variables cited must be clearly defined. The supporting evidence must go beyond single and local observations, ideally approaching a complete sampling of all relevant situations.

Much of our knowledge about intergroup relations is derived from *cumulative* evidence. There are few propositions in this field which are supported by the clear-cut evidence of the crucial experiment or the situation of the crucial difference. Rather, their plausibility rests upon the agreement or mutually interlocking character of many observations made over a wide range of circumstances. Because of difficulties of observation and experimental control, this type of evidence probably will continue to be the dominant one.

Beyond such considerations of formal proof, the kind of evidence needed in this field has certain other specifications. Above all, it must be *important*. To meet this criterion the evidence must bear upon either a key point of scientific theory, or a matter having significant social implications. There are problems which meet both tests, and some which qualify on only one, but at least one count of significance should be met.

Furthermore, it is not too much to ask that studies be designed to contribute to systematic theory. Chapters III and IV will go into some detail on the problems and possibilities involved in this requirement. It is enough at this point to indicate that our crucial need is not so much for isolated "new data" as for studies whose significance is mutually reinforced by being placed in a framework of interrelated theory.

Review of Representative Research Findings

It has been shown that activities designed to control and guide inter-group relations are widespread and intensive. Certain criteria have been suggested for judging the evidence required to appraise the results of these efforts. What, then, is actually known from systematic research on the effects of action in this field?

If attention is restricted to published studies using quantitative methods, we find that the available data apply almost entirely to the effects of relatively brief and limited stimuli. The available studies have been classified by Arnold Rose [28] into these groups:

1. Studies of effectiveness of school courses dealing with race relations
2. Studies of effectiveness of specific propaganda
3. Studies of effectiveness of personal contacts
4. Studies of change in attitude not objectively measured
5. Correlational studies of attitude vs. knowledge of or contact with minorities
6. Studies of differential effectiveness of media of communication
7. Studies of differential effectiveness of logical vs. emotional propaganda
8. Studies of differential effects of prestige symbols
9. Studies of differential effectiveness of techniques of using a given medium of mass communication

In order to avoid duplication of the summarization prepared by Rose, this discussion will be limited to a brief over-all view of the evidence.

Table I is a summary of representative studies of changes in intergroup attitudes and their findings. The studies reported here exclude numerous static-descriptive efforts. Although there are some outstanding exceptions, it can be agreed in general: "The literature in this field, until very recently, shows a narrow emphasis on the surface aspects of the problem; . . . Descriptive data of a static variety constitute the major proportions [of the data obtained]." [29] Table I is restricted to research which deals with *changes* or with correlational analysis aimed at the discovery of factors in change.

As Table II indicates *the weight of the evidence from published studies is that the stimuli tested* (school and college courses, specific propaganda, personal contacts, information, and general education) *do result in or are accompanied by attitude changes in a "positive" direction.* On the other hand, nearly half of the studies have found inconclusive

---

[28] *Studies in Reduction of Prejudice* (Chicago: American Council on Race Relations, 1947, mimeographed).
[29] Lippitt and Radke, *op. cit.*, p. 167.

TABLE I. REPRESENTATIVE STUDIES OF CHANGES IN INTERGROUP ATTITUDES: BEFORE-AND-AFTER TESTING

| Investigator (and bibliographical citation *) | Type of study | | Number of cases | Subjects | Influences tested | Techniques of observation or measurement | Findings |
	Experimental and control groups	Before-and-after testing of experimental groups					
1. D. Young (218)		X	450	College undergraduates	Course in race relations	Ranking of ethnic groups	No change in relative position of groups ranked
2. D. Young (216)		X	16	Graduate students	Visit to Negro Hospital; participation in activities there	Own questionnaire; psychological examination	Slight increase in tolerance, but results inconclusive
3. Schlorff (187)	X		425	High-school students	15 weeks course aimed to increase tolerance toward the Negro	Paired comparisons (Thurstone method) of 20 nationalities; social distance scale	No change in control group. Experimental group ranked the Negro higher at end than at beginning of course
4. Droba (58)		X	30	College students	Course on the Negro	Hinckley scale, A and B	No change (slight favorable tendency)
5. Wanger (206)		X	40	High-school students	Course including material on Negroes	Written testimony; direct observation (no objective tests)	More favorable toward Negroes at end of course

Study			Number	Population	Treatment	Tests	Results
6. Campbell and Stover (30)	X	X	48 (24 with paired controls)	9th grade girls	Study of Negro; experimental factor: use of opaque projector	Tests: Bogardus, Hinckley, Neumann-Kulpmann-Davidson	More favorable on Bogardus test, but not on the Hinckley scale
7. Manske (132)		X	28 (14 with paired controls)	9th grade boys	Instruction on 10 races for one group; other group studied 10 other races	Bogardus	Positive for one group; inconclusive for the other
			661	High-school students	"Non-indoctrinating" lessons by teachers with "liberal" and "prejudiced" attitudes	Hinckley	Of 22 classes tested, only 2 changed in direction of the teacher's attitude; 8 changed in opposite direction
8. Bolton (20 and 21)	X		162	Women college students	Study of Negro education	Hinckley	No significant change
9. Ford (65)		X	26	College students	Course in immigration and race relations	Bogardus; Hinckley; own scale of experience	Positive shift in attitude; no change in reported experience
10. Billings (14)		X	26	College students	Seminar on social problems	"Scale of Belief"	Slight increase in "favorable" attitudes
11. M. Smith (194)	X		81 (46 in one group; 35 in other)	College students	Course in immigration and race problems	Bogardus; Hinckley	Slight "favorable" gain; considerable shifting of individuals, positive and negative
12. F. T. Smith (193)	X		354 (exp. and control groups, 46)	Graduate students	Tour and visit in Harlem	Battery of tests, including Hinckley	Significant gain in favorableness of attitudes toward Negroes

* See the Selected Bibliography, pp. 135–145, *infra*.

Investigator (and bibliographical citation*)	Type of study — Experimental and control groups	Type of study — Before-and-after testing of experimental groups	Number of cases	Subjects	Influences tested	Techniques of observation or measurement	Findings
13. Brooks (26)		X (Quasi-control group)	238	Sociology students (college)	Course with special study of race	Modified Bogardus (on 12 ethnic groups)	No significant change. Tests showed preference for better-educated members of ethnic groups
14. Remmers (171)		X	300	High-school students	One class period of pro-Negro indoctrination	Generalized scale of attitude toward any social group	More favorable to Negro
15. Chen (35 and 36)	X		662 (3 control and 6 exp. groups)	College students	Pro-Chinese, pro-Japanese and neutral propaganda (oral)	Agreement with 20 statements on Manchurian issue	Significant changes in direction of each propaganda appeal
16. Peterson and Thurstone (161)		X	130	School children (grades 7–12)	Motion picture: "Four Sons" (pro-German)	Thurstone tests	More favorable to Germans
17. Idem (161)		X	180	School children (grades 9–12)	Motion picture "Son of Gods" (favorable to Chinese)	Thurstone tests	More favorable to Chinese
18. Idem (161)		X	434	School children (grades 6–12)	Motion picture "Birth of a Nation" (anti-Negro)	Thurstone tests	Less favorable to Negroes

* See the Selected Bibliography, pp. 135–145, *infra*.

results or no change in attitudes. No important attitude changes in a negative (more prejudiced) direction have been reported, although some boomerang effects were noted in a few studies (e.g., F. T. Smith's and W. K-C. Chen's).

TABLE II. NUMBER OF STUDIES SHOWING CHANGES OR LACK OF CHANGE AS A RESULT OF SPECIFIC INFLUENCES *

Influences	Change ("more favorable")	No change	Indefinite	Total
School or college course	6	4	1	11
Specific propaganda	7	1	1	9
Personal contacts	3	3	2	8
Knowledge or acquaintance (correlations)	7	2	1	10
Time in school	8	6	4	18
Total	31	16	9	56

* Adapted from Rose, *op. cit.*

Thus, considerable work has been done to determine whether attitudes are changed by given programs; on the other hand, the differential effectiveness of various media and techniques in influencing intergroup attitudes and behavior has received very little research attention. Appraisal of the effectiveness of alternative possibilities is a crucial need in all intergroup work, but thus far it can be made for the most part only by analogy from general work on communication and propaganda.

In the few experimental studies the following findings have been reported: [30]

1. Auditory stimuli are more effective than visual stimuli. (F. R. Elliott, 60; W. H. Wilke, 213)[31]
2. Speakers are more effective than printed matter. (F. R. Elliott, 60; W. H. Wilke, 213; not found by B. M. Cherrington and L. W. Miller, 37)
3. "Emotional" appeals tend to be more effective than "logical" appeals, but there are exceptions. (G. W. Hartmann, 83; no difference in effects shown by F. H. Knower, 107)

It has been suggested that indirect or emotional appeals are likely to be less effective than direct rational arguments when the audience is well educated or initially convinced of views contrary to the position taken in the propaganda.

[30] It must be stressed that the findings as stated apply only to the specific materials and situations tested in the particular studies cited.

[31] Names and numbers in parentheses refer to items in the Selected Bibliography, pp. 135–145, *infra*.

4. Oral propaganda is more effective in small groups than in large audiences. (F. H. Knower, 107)
5. The effectiveness of propaganda tends to be greater when the material is linked with prestige symbols. (I. Lorge, 129; M. Saadi and P. R. Farnsworth, 183; C. H. Marple, 135, and many others)

These further suggestions have been advanced on the basis of limited evidence: [32]

1. The use of several channels of communication simultaneously is more effective than the use of only one medium.
2. Pictures and cartoons have greater attention-gaining value than the written word and are more effective in conveying a message, except in the case of complex and abstract ideas.
3. In a series of presentations of materials each item of which tends to produce an effect in the same direction, each successive presentation has less effect than the first.

So far as can be discovered at this writing, there are no published studies which demonstrate the differential effectiveness in intergroup relations of various media, or of techniques of presentation, or of types of appeals. There has been some unpublished research, e.g., testing effectiveness of cartoons, but research findings on the specific problems confronting action agencies in their daily education and propaganda activities are not generally available.

Over fifty studies have been reviewed in the brief analysis above. They represent a considerable amount of effort, and in many instances they were made with all the thoughtfulness and care possible within the limitations of the situations confronted by the investigators. Yet the findings are largely inadequate as aids in matters of everyday decision and practice in action programs. From these findings *we surely know that some kinds of communication and contact are accompanied by changes in opinion which indicate lessened prejudice.* This result should not be discounted, either as "an elaboration of the obvious" or as unimportant; for it is important to know that such changes in opinion can be induced and, in the absence of such studies as these, it is by no means self-evident that attempts to change opinions have the intended outcomes. Nevertheless, existing research knowledge is unsatisfactory because it is fragmentary, and consequently can not supply the dependable aids to action which are potentially realizable.

[32] See the statements by Arnold Rose, S. H. Flowerman and others in American Council on Race Relations, *Summary: Public Relations Workshop, September 27-8-9, 1946* (Chicago, 1947).

Two shortcomings of the available studies are striking because of their obviousness: (a) there are not nearly enough of them; (b) they have not been geared into a systematic exploration of the strategic problem-areas. The sheer paucity of individual research projects means that there is not that extensive repetition of observations which is essential for establishing scientific generalizations in all fields of study—and especially in this, because of the complexity of the problems and the difficulties in control of factors.[33] The second point follows in part from the first since the limited number of investigations inevitably has involved neglect of some problems in favor of others, rather than a well-rounded coverage of the field. Part of the difficulty arises also from inadequate attention to systematic theory, on the one hand, and from incomplete awareness of the needs of social action and social policy, on the other. Chapter III suggests that there already exists a guiding framework of theory which is reasonably adequate as a tentative point of departure, subject of course to revisions in further study and research. It is believed, furthermore, that the rapidly growing rapprochement of social science and action programs may furnish the other set of guiding influences necessary for a more complete and meaningfully integrated research program.

Beyond these broad inadequacies the present inventory shows a number of more specific deficiencies. First, most studies have been limited to small samples. Of 32 representative studies of attitude change, 11 included less than 100 cases and only 4 had 500 or more cases. With such small groups statistical reliabilities are so low that findings must often be inconclusive, whether a real change is being recorded or not. Perhaps equally important is the fact that the studies were concerned exclusively with school or college students. A third limitation is that so many studies have worked only with correlations or with before-and-after measurement without a control group: of 32 studies reviewed, only 6 measured changes in both experimental and control groups.[34]

When we ask why these deficiencies in existing research materials have been tolerated in the face of motives, skills, and knowledge counter to their acceptance, one major explanation seems inescapable: Support for research and research training in this field has been so inadequate that the necessary improvements often could not be made, no matter

---

[33] For a fuller discussion of these points, see Chapter IV and the Appendix.

[34] This is not meant to imply that every study must have a pure experimental design, nor that correlation studies can not yield causal inferences. However, control groups are not used in many instances in which the procedure is technically feasible and would strengthen the proof.

how sincere the desire to achieve them. This is certainly a chief reason for the concentration on small samples of student populations—groups which could be studied on the local campus at small expense.

Four other points which are properly subject to critical review may be briefly summarized:

(1) Most of the studies of projected change have tested the effects of stimuli which were of relatively brief duration—a lecture, a motion picture, visiting minority group members, a college course—and which were probably relatively minor in relation to other influences in the subject's social milieu. The ofttimes slight and inconclusive changes recorded may reflect these facts. There is a need for studies covering more extensive and intensive *programs of influences as wholes,* e.g., a "barrage" of the techniques judged best on a priori grounds should be applied to test the maximum effects which could be expected under the best current practices. Also, in spite of the increased difficulties of experimental control, follow-up studies to measure retention of changes over longer periods might be worth while. (A retest after six months is about the maximum period usually reported.)

(2) Considerable improvement in the *adequacy of descriptions of stimuli and the context of their application* appears feasible. Often we are told little more, for example, than that students were "given a 10 weeks course in race relations." There is little description of texts and other materials, teaching techniques used, student backgrounds, relevant local events, the instructor's attitudes and purposes, and similar pertinent factors. Specific descriptions along these lines are essential both for repetitive studies and for meaningful comparisons of findings reported by different investigators.

(3) Past studies have sometimes used measuring or ranking devices which have been superseded by more recent developments in research technique. For example, certain widely used scales of attitude toward minority groups are definitely suspect; new methods are available for construction of uni-dimensional scales; most simple rating tests should be set aside except for very special and limited purposes.[35]

(4) Finally, a conspicuous fact about past research on attempts to change intergroup relations is the preponderance of measurement of verbalizations (opinions) *in isolation from other behavior.* This is an area of omission of relevant data in which considerable improvement is desirable and possible (Cf. Appendix, pp. 114 ff.).

---

[35] For more complete treatment of this subject, see the section on research techniques in the Appendix, pp. 112 ff.

By way of review, Chapter I sketched the general setting of inter-group problems in the United States. Chapter II has surveyed some of the problems of programs aimed at amelioration and control, examined research evidence as to the effects of attempts to change intergroup attitudes, and indicated certain crucial deficiencies in the available studies. In Chapter III, attention will be turned to the questions upon which further evidence is needed. Only after the strategic hypotheses have been reviewed, will we be in a position to consider the potentially productive research approaches which may throw light on some of the more significant and vexing questions.

CHAPTER III

PROPOSITIONS ON INTERGROUP HOSTILITY AND CONFLICT

Preliminary Considerations

In any research on problems of intergroup relations it is essential to distinguish at least three aspects of negative interaction: prejudice (hostility), discrimination, and conflict. Although often closely connected in life situations, these elements have a considerable range of independent variation. Accordingly, the implied therapies are not necessarily the same when the aim is, e.g., to remove prejudice as when it is merely to minimize conflict.

In its broadest meaning prejudice may be considered simply as a *prejudgment* of individuals on the basis of some type of social categorization. A prejudice is thus a generalization which operates in advance of the particular situation in which it is manifested. An illustration is a stereotype which attributes a cluster of traits to individuals as representative of a group; it is thus in one aspect a cluster of cognitive judgments, implying a set of behavioral expectations. In another aspect it involves a set of evaluations. That is, the prejudice is not simply a set of expectations; it is also a set of evaluations of good and bad, superior and inferior. Thus a prejudiced individual brings to the immediate situation certain beliefs as to the traits of others, coupled with a positive or negative predisposition toward these traits.

Prejudice, in this general sense, is an inevitable and universal feature of social life. What is significant as a variable is the basis upon which any particular prejudice rests. The crucial distinction lies between prejudices which are based upon functional position in the social order or real differences in values, and those which emphasize stereotypes centered on symbols such as skin color which have no intrinsic functional importance. Thus, all prejudices represent action-sets of a categorical rather than situational or ad hoc character. But there is a great difference between "prejudices" against social positions such as employers, ministers, labor leaders, radio commentators, bootleggers, professors, landlords, etc., on the one hand, and prejudices against racial or cultural groups, on the other.

The particular type of prejudice which is important in understanding hostility and conflict among ethnic, racial, or religious groups is *a negative attitude which violates some important norms or values nominally accepted in the culture.* As a matter of fact, group prejudice has been defined as "a common attitude of hostile nature whose manifestations conflict with some aspects of the basic value framework of the society in which they occur."[1]

Even in this narrower meaning prejudice is a blanket concept, covering a variety of concrete phenomena. The prejudice may be mild or violent. There is a contrast between prejudice manifested against groups with whom one has had no personal contact, and against those with whom contact is intensive and continuous. There is the prejudice of the provincial—to anything strange, different, "foreign"—and the rather different prejudice of the dweller in cosmopolitan centers. We may note in this connection that anthropologists have been able to make predictions about the behavior of nonliterate tribes in contact with Europeans simply on the basis of the absence of certain behavior patterns in the native culture. There is perhaps a closely analogous situation in the cases of persons who have spent their entire lives in communities with definite patterns of intergroup discrimination and prejudice. A radically different pattern is unknown; they have neither the motivations nor the social skills to deal with intergroup relations except in accordance with the traditional patterns of their local social system. Even with a large fund of "good will" such persons may be expected to show awkwardness, insecurity, and erratic shifts in behavior (and its accompanying affects) when they attempt to act in ways foreign to the accustomed and sanctioned modes. Prejudice in this context is certainly not the same concrete phenomenon as the "deliberate" prejudice of the sophisticated urbanite.

Again, there is prejudice based on conformity to the social customs of a group as against the prejudice, anchored in deep aggressive needs in the personality, which may persist even in the face of group pressure. There is the prejudice of economic or political opportunism, often calculating and impersonal, in contrast to the fanaticism of the religious or cultural zealot. There is the prejudice manifest in a specific idée fixe concerning a particular group, on the one hand, and the prejudice expressive of generalized antipathy to out-groups, on the other. Even the prejudice which arises primarily out of individual psychological needs appears in many forms; it may serve, for example, as a projection of repressed hatreds and other "antisocial" urges of the individual, a prop

[1] G. H. Grosser and S. J. Korchin, "Some Theoretical Aspects of Group Prejudice and Conflict" (mimeographed paper from the Harvard University Seminar on Group Prejudice and Conflict, fall term, 1944–45), p. 2.

for ego-level or sense of self-esteem, a defense against repressed sexual drives, or a method of winning group approval.[2]

Furthermore, although prejudice is often analyzed as if it were a unitary phenomenon—essentially the same whatever the particular groups in question—we are not yet convinced that this basic assumption has been proven valid. For example, Ichheiser[3] has presented a rather plausible case for the view that anti-Negro and anti-Jewish prejudices are partly based upon, or at least "rationalized" in terms of, different sensed threats. His argument is, in part, that "fear of the gangster" is the more important component in the case of anti-Negro feeling whereas "fear of fraud" is dominant in the anti-Semitic complex. This suggestion needs further refining and testing,[4] but there is much evidence that the specific content of prejudice against Negroes differs from that against Jews, and these in turn from that against Catholics.[5] To take only one illustration, a major theme for rationalizing anti-Negro feeling has been that of alleged intellectual incapacities or general biological inferiority; but one of the important elements in anti-Jewish stereotypes is just the opposite, namely, an emphasis upon alleged mental agility, shrewdness, and competitive success.

Our emphasis upon the fact that the concepts of prejudice or hostility merit further analytical dissection is by no means merely a matter of verbal quibbles, for the definition of the concepts inevitably involves different modes of action. If it were assumed that prejudice against each of the various minorities in the United States is "the same thing," it might be decided, for instance, that one line of therapy would be to furnish information about a group's accomplishments and to disseminate propaganda stressing the distinguished individuals in the group. Would the results be the same for Jews as for Negroes? For Mexican Americans as for Japanese? Or, suppose prejudice is conceived so broadly as to imply no difference between the prejudice of an Ozark farmer in a county having no Negroes in its population, and the prejudice of an Alabama planter in the Black Belt. It is surely possible that a program

[2] Cf. Fritz Redl's discussion in *Intercultural Education News*, 7(4):3–5 (1946); also, G. W. Allport, *A B C's of Scapegoating* (Chicago: Central Y. M. C. A. College), pp. 15–23.

[3] Gustav Ichheiser, "Fear of Violence and Fear of Fraud," *Sociometry*, 7:376–383 (1944).

[4] Allport and Kramer report that students who said they were more afraid of "swindlers" than of "gangsters" had higher prejudice scores *in general*. The authors suggest that a "suspicious philosophy of life" goes along with greater generalized prejudice toward outgroups. ("Some Roots of Prejudice," *Journal of Psychology*, 22:9–39)

[5] Studies reviewed by Arnold Rose (*Studies in Reduction of Prejudice, op. cit.*) indicate that changes in attitude toward a given minority group are not necessarily transferred to attitudes toward other minorities.

of amelioration based on this conception would have different results in the two cases. And to the degree that such differences may be anticipated, research needs and possibilities become clearer and more significant.

It is clear from comparative study of situations involving intergroup relations that prejudice is not perfectly correlated with discrimination or conflict. Discrimination in some degree always accompanies prejudice, but a given state of prejudice may be accompanied by greatly varying degrees and types of discrimination. The latter may be generally defined as the *differential treatment of individuals considered to belong to a particular social group*. Like prejudice, discrimination in this sense is an inevitable and universal feature of social life. The social groups may or may not have a biological basis, and if they have, the biological referents may or may not be functional. The "discrimination" against women in public life, for example, is based in part on a biologically functional referent. Discrimination against Negroes, on the other hand, is based upon the culturally imputed significance of certain traits such as skin color which have no demonstrated relevance to biological function. Again, there is discrimination against religious, occupational, ethnic, and other groups which have no real or assumed biological referents. To arrive at a definitive view of discrimination it must be pointed out that in the context of intergroup relations the word ordinarily refers not merely to selective or differential behavior, but to such behavior *insofar as it violates important institutional standards* which usually are obligatory in certain areas of conduct. Thus, except for the probable deviations around such social norms, it is expected in our society that occupational opportunity will be available on the basis of merit or ability, that all citizens are entitled to specified legal rights, that economic transactions will be carried out according to the rules of the market. Discrimination may be said to exist to the degree that individuals of a given group who are otherwise formally qualified are not treated in conformity with these nominally universal institutionalized codes.

A high level of active hostility shading into open intergroup *conflict* is still a third type of problem, not necessarily coextensive with the other two. Prejudice unquestionably is sharpest just prior to, during, and sometimes immediately after a conflict situation. But prejudice may exist in the absence of direct contact between groups, as formerly against the "terrible Turk" when there was no actual opportunity for direct conflict. Also, it must be remembered that a firmly established caste system, which in some respects represents a maximum of prejudice, may operate with little open conflict.[6]

Now, taking conflict alone as the final expression of prejudice-hostility, we may distinguish at least three major types of "realistic" conflict, which differ in their bases of origin: conflict of interests, of values (cultural conflict), of personality types.[7] Any intergroup conflict ordinarily involves all three types in varying proportions. With groups which are already culturally identified by clear symbols, the competition of members of the different groups for wealth, work, power, and various symbols of status and success defines a "realistic" conflict of interests. Similarly, there are often real intergroup differences in values, beliefs, personal habits, and customs. Such cultural differences may and often do lead to tangible disagreements on matters of considerable emotional importance to individuals; and both parties may be convinced of the rightness of their own positions. Third, because of varying modal patterns of family conditioning and perhaps other factors, different groups may contain different proportions of various personality types—a fact which does not appear to be wholly reducible to differences in the formal content of group culture. Insofar as such differences exist, interpersonal contacts may lead to irritation, hostility, and conflict.

In addition to these three main bases of "realistic" conflict, group hostility typically involves certain "unrealistic" components. At least three may be considered to have practical importance: ignorance and error, deflected hostility, historical tradition.

The influence of ignorance is widely recognized and is the object of much educational effort. Sheer unawareness of other groups' characteristics, especially lack of acquaintance with individuals, is conducive to exaggeration of intergroup differences and to receptivity to hostile propaganda. Erroneous judgments may be made even with fairly complete knowledge, if incorrect inferences are drawn from known facts. This is especially important in the case of imputations of "responsi-

[6] This example is enough to demonstrate that the mere minimization of *conflict* alone is not the goal of most groups concerned with intergroup relations in the United States. The problem is much more complicated. What many representatives of minority groups are actually seeking is a minimum of prejudice, together with a minimum of conflict, and a minimum of discrimination. At least in the short run, these objectives are not necessarily mutually compatible. For instance, the attempt to eliminate discrimination often leads directly to increases in hostility and conflict; efforts to avoid conflict, conversely, may perpetuate or reinforce patterns of discrimination.

[7] Adapted from Gustav Ichheiser, "The Jews and Anti-Semitism," *Sociometry,* 9:92–108 (1946).

bility," e.g., when a decline in material rewards arising from complex forces in our economic system is imputed to specific groups which do not have any significant causal role in the situation.

Deflected hostility takes two main forms: projection and displacement. In the first, unacceptable elements in the personality are attributed to others; thus it is the other group which is said to be hostile, or scheming to exploit, and so on. In the second, hostility is directed against a source other than that which originally created it. In intergroup relations deflected hostility may result in "overdetermined" reactions in which the hostility is out of all proportion to the realistic basis. This situation depends upon a complex set of factors (see Proposition 8, p. 52, *infra*), but an essential element is the existence of much hostility which can not be directly expressed or otherwise dissipated within the groups in which it originates. The persistence and virulence of intergroup hostility is certainly not explicable without taking deflected aggression into account.

The factor of historical tradition must be accorded the status of a variable. Old rivalries, conflicts, and traumas are remembered, and traditional prejudices may tend to be perpetuated well beyond the point at which they cease to have any intrinsic relevance to current situations.

To appraise the relative importance of realistic and unrealistic components or of interests versus values in intergroup tension would be a very hazardous undertaking at the present stage of our understanding, although such appraisals are often given with surprising confidence and conviction. We can be reasonably sure, however, that any explanation of intergroup hostility in terms of a single factor like "purely economic competition" represents an oversimplification which is likely to encourage ill conceived action. Further, the known facts create a strong presumption that a main source of the persistence of intergroup hostility is precisely the *interlocking and mutual reinforcement* of cultural differences, other visible differences, realistic interests, deflected aggression, and other factors. In short, the most important questions may concern not the influence of particular factors but the way in which mutual reinforcement operates, and determination of the strategic factors in a plan for shifting the resultant pattern. In this connection, there is a definite possibility that the factors which are most important in producing hostility and conflict are by no means the same as those which are most important *for control purposes*. Thus, the roots of intergroup hostility may lie in the early socialization of children in the home. But this process is so inaccessible to direct external control that other, even seemingly far removed, approaches may be much more promising for immediate action.

Such considerations as those sketched above are essential to fruitful orientation of research on techniques for reducing or controlling intergroup hostility. They indicate clearly, for example, that action programs may deal with either realistic or unrealistic components or both, and that the predicted effects may be expected to vary with the choices made. To take another application, the present analysis implies that even complete intergroup knowledge could not by itself eliminate group hostility. It implies, also, that indirect approaches which attack the realistic bases of conflict, perhaps without even ostensibly dealing with intergroup relations as such, have as valid a claim for consideration as do direct education or propaganda approaches.

Definitions

In view of the need for rigorous conceptual distinctions, indicated in the preceding paragraphs, it is obligatory here to define the usages of certain key terms which will be followed in the remainder of the discussion. There probably is not as yet any one best definition for some of these terms; the usefulness of a particular definition often depends upon the context in which it is to be applied. Accordingly, the present formulations [8] are regarded as tentative and there is no presumption of universal applicability:

1. *Ethnic group:* one possessing continuity through biological descent whose members share a distinctive social and cultural tradition
2. *Racial group:* one whose members through biological descent share distinctive common hereditary physical characteristics
3. *Religious group:* one whose members share a common orientation (set of beliefs and values) toward real or imaginary things and events considered to be outside the area of ordinary human practice and control
4. *Group prejudice:* a common (shared) attitude of hostile nature toward a social group, whose manifestations conflict with some aspects of the basic value framework of the society in which they occur
5. *Group hostility:* a common (shared) attitude, as defined by verbal and nonverbal acts, which consists of tendencies to insult, disparage, ostracize, deprive, threaten, or inflict other physical or social injuries upon members of a social group *by virtue of membership therein*

[8] These definitions have been markedly influenced by the discussions of Grosser and Korchin, *op. cit.,* and Talcott Parsons, "Racial and Religious Differences as Factors in Group Tensions," in L. Bryson, L. Finkelstein and R. M. MacIver, eds., *Approaches to National Unity* (New York: Harper & Brothers, 1945), pp. 182–199.

6. *Group discrimination:* the differential treatment of individuals, insofar as this is based upon their membership in a given social group, which conflicts with important institutional rules within a society

7. *Competition:* a continuing struggle for scarce, distributive values in which the focus is upon reaching a goal rather than removing competitors, and which is regulated by rules prohibiting forceful removal of competitors. It may be completely impersonal and outside personal awareness.

8. *Conflict:* a struggle over values (distributive or nondistributive) in which the immediate aims of the opponents are to neutralize, injure, or eliminate their rivals. Conflict results from the conscious pursuit of exclusive values.

9. *Aggression:* an act whose end is the belief that injury to or destruction of a person or his values and symbols has been achieved [9]

Major Theorems

The design of research as well as the planning of action in the field of relations among ethnic, religious, and racial groups may well be guided in broadest orientation by several of the most general postulates in social science. Those of most direct relevance include:

1. The principles of multiple causation of social events and of the interdependence of variables in a system
2. The theorem of cumulation in social change
3. The principle of limits in social change
4. The principle of indirection in guided action aimed at planned social change.

Each of these principles or postulates has a number of implications for research and other purposive action.

Intergroup hostility furnishes especially apt illustrations of multiple effects. Any single instance of group hostility can be shown to have many important causes from which multiple consequences ensue. Furthermore, each of the most important factors is interrelated with several others in a state of mutual dependence such that a change in one variable alters the values of others.[10]

To take a hypothetical case, we may suppose that the causal factors in an urban race riot can be shown to include at least the following: (1) a high level of frustration arising from poor housing, low incomes,

---

[9] Suggested by the somewhat different definition of John Dollard and others in *Frustration and Aggression* (New Haven: Yale University Press, 1939).

[10] This definitely does not mean that all variables are assumed to be equally important. The specific weight to be given each factor is a matter for determination in each specific situation.

excessive crowding of transportation systems and other public facilities, lack of satisfying recreation, disruption of family life and community membership; (2) patterns of prejudice of complex origin established prior to the immediate situation; (3) a rapid change in relative numbers of the two contending groups; (4) a lack of intergroup familiarity because of segregation and other factors; (5) a rapid differential change in incomes of the two groups; (6) the presence of "hoodlum" elements emerging from prior social disorganization; (7) the presence of opportunistic leaders who can advance their private interests through encouraging conflict; (8) absence of adequate, well trained, well organized, and relatively impartial law-enforcement forces. In the total situation each of these factors may be a necessary condition but no one of them may be sufficient to account for the occurrence of a riot in just the way it actually happened. The factors may be mutually related, as when segregation interacts with prejudice, or the relative income levels affect competition for housing, or the absence of certain recreational patterns increases "hoodlum" activity, or prejudice influences the character of the law-enforcement agencies.

This hypothetical case shows how a comparatively few variables may be combined in a most complex system of interrelations. Such complex interdependence often leads to various indirect and unanticipated or "boomerang" effects of specific actions. Insofar as the theorems of multiple causation and of interdependence of variables are valid, they have at least these implications:

(a) The effects of isolated actions or programs are likely to be small. Frequently these effects will be attenuated, obscured, or reversed by other factors operative in the total situation.

(b) The effects of a given action or program are not necessarily confined to the most direct or obviously related areas. Both research and action must be sensitized to the possibility of repercussions which are indirect and far reaching.

(c) Other things being equal, programs of action are likely to have greatest effects when they operate simultaneously on several strategic factors, rather than upon one or a few.

(d) Causal inferences must be made with great care, and in the light of all the possibly relevant known factors.

(e) Panaceas for control of group hostility definitely will not be found.

The theorem of cumulation in social change, essentially as set forth by Myrdal,[11] provides a useful orientation with certain qualifications.

[11] *An American Dilemma,* pp. 1065–1070.

The principle is that a given social system may be conveniently regarded as an unstable equilibrium, in which a relatively slight change in a given direction tends to set off a chain of effects which cumulate to produce a larger change than the immediate consequences of the initial alteration. Given a set of factors tending to produce group hostility, there sometimes thus arises a "vicious circle" of reactions tending to intensify and spread hostility. A relatively inconspicuous reversal of the "cycle" in regard to a strategic factor, conversely, under some circumstances will establish a cumulative tendency to re-equilibration involving a decrease in hostility and conflict.

The most important reservation with respect to this theorem is based upon that of multiple-interdependent variables, and upon the principle of limits. The latter is really the explicit formulation of a common-sense observation: Social systems are not indefinitely plastic but have inherent (although rather wide) functional limits to variation. Thus, the cumulation of effects is checked by broad functional limits, e.g., need for a certain amount of order, beyond which a given system can not go without disruption. Also, the pyramiding of consequences may be complicated, stopped, or reversed by indirect effects upon other mutually dependent variables. Thus, cumulation is not a simple mechanical process but involves dynamic and functional equilibrium. It is important to recognize that the direction of end effects is not necessarily the same as that of the initial impetus. Furthermore, a given line of development may have one series of consequences at one stage, and different or even opposite concomitants at later stages. Thus, Myrdal gives the example of a rising educational level among Southern Negroes as a factor tending to reverse the "vicious circle." It is quite conceivable that under certain circumstances the reactions of the white population to this factor might follow this sequence: (1) Initial resistance and hostility would be followed by (2) acceptance of a higher level of education and of the correlated socio-economic claims. (3) If still higher average educational levels were sought, there might be a new reaction of hostility, as the more crucial blockages of a caste-like system were challenged. (4) A new level of accommodation *or* a reversion to former patterns would ensue, with important secondary repercussions.

Finally, the interdependence of factors in human relations usually precludes simple mechanical substitutions. To remove aggression against one "scapegoat" under some conditions would result in the appearance of a new scapegoat, but this would almost certainly bring about other important changes at the same time. Thus, from the fact that laws enforcing segregation in some cases seem to have increased intergroup hostility, it does not necessarily follow that repeal of the legislation would simply reverse the process.

The principle of indirection is applicable in any field of social action in which direct manipulation of causal factors for bringing about a given change is blocked by predictable emotional reactions arising from elements in the social structure. It is particularly indicated when the problem is that of changing crystallized emotional tendencies or customary behavior patterns of individuals. In such situations direct attempts to change attitudes or behavior patterns tend to be perceived by the recipients as attacks. The typical immediate reaction is a mobilization of defensive personality functions and an intensification of the original pattern. In this type of situation, which is perhaps usual in many areas of intergroup relations, the most promising approach is often that of instituting processes which undercut the basis of the undesired behavior. An illustration might be the provision of employment in which Negroes and whites came in contact under favorable working conditions, including satisfactory incomes, common interests, and the like. The "race issue" might not be raised at all, but the resulting group relations might represent appreciable changes in attitudes. Similarly, if the isolation and poverty of certain white groups are important in creating attitudes of support for a rigid caste-like system in the rural South, a long-term program of industrialization and improvement of facilities for communication and mobility might do more to reduce hostility between Negroes and whites in these areas than elaborate attempts at education and propaganda.

The use of indirect rather than frontal approaches in a given situation often implies a wish to minimize conflict. Whether an action program should strive to avoid a certain intensity of conflict in order to reach a given end is a problem of value judgment outside the scope of this monograph. Every action of any kind, including failure to act, "costs something." A considerable measure of conflict is often part of the price of any extensive or rapid gain in status on the part of a traditional minority, even under the most favorable circumstances which can be expected in practice. The principle of indirection means, in part, that action programs which aim to minimize any increased intergroup hostility arising from carrying out their other purposes must analyze the social structure to find strategic points of leverage, and areas of flexibility in which intergroup solidarity may be established, as points of departure for later action.

It is apparent from the preceding analysis that *to be most effective, research on approaches for reducing intergroup hostility must be oriented in terms of the total social system in which it operates.* The relation between this simple and apparently vague postulate and specific research problems can be clarified by a brief examination of certain recent trends in social science.

Most of the early research in the United States on intergroup relations was static, descriptive, and atomistic. The aim was usually to describe and measure the degree or incidence of prejudice of individuals. Prejudice and hostility were often conceived almost wholly in terms of stereotypes and motives which were treated *as if* individuals were the only significant units in social systems. Studies on this level were almost wholly divorced from social surveys, from analyses of economic conditions, legal structure and power relations, and other broad formal types of investigation. From this situation one route to interdisciplinary integration, and to sounder appreciation of the roles of social structure and personality needs, came through a genetic approach, specifically in studies of socialization of the child and the resulting recognition that group prejudices were somehow acquired in the process. Meanwhile, studies of personality dynamics and emotional structuring were demonstrating some of the sources of aggressive needs in the individual, and analyzing the complicated intrapersonal mechanisms for dealing with hostile urges. These results were available to sociologists and anthropologists, who had been accumulating a mass of observations on variations in social structure, on the patterning of institutional behavior, and on the integrating factors in group dynamics. All these lines of influence, together with several others, could hardly fail to bring recognition of the need for synthesis and new orientation.

Reformulations of theory and new demonstrations of fact have rapidly opened up new leads. For example, recent studies have specifically demonstrated the importance of *group membership* for social perception [12] and attitude change. Experimental evidence now substantiates the common-sense hunch that individuals are more resistant to change if supported by a group, and that changed attitudes are stabilized by membership in a group sharing the change.[13] The concrete social group as a variable in behavior has found a place in psychological experimenta-

[12] For example, M. Sherif, *The Psychology of Social Norms* (New York: Harper & Brothers, 1936).
[13] K. Lewin and P. Grabbe, "Conduct, Knowledge, and Acceptance of New Values," *Journal of Social Issues,* 1(3):53–64 (1945).

tion, as it has long been prominent in sociological and anthropological thought.

With similar import, numerous studies have accumulated evidence that hostility and conflict vary greatly in intensity and nature in different sectors of a given society, and in different social systems taken as wholes. Many of these variations have been meaningfully related to variations in the institutional framework characteristic of such sectors or systems. Comparative studies of cooperation and competition in various cultures have highlighted the intense competition in our own mobile society, and have yielded implications for the study of intergroup dynamics.

The scientific discovery of culture has likewise taken its place in what promises to be a real transformation of basic theory. Human behavior has come to be seen in relation to the pervasive patterns of social heredity which face each new generation, and a fresh appreciation of structural regularities is widely manifest. This development has come in a period marked by strong repudiation of "single factor" theories of action, and by a corresponding willingness to think in terms of multiple and inter-acting variables.

The time is ripe for incorporation of these productive trends in con-crete research. Furthermore, the field of intergroup relations most clearly illustrates the need for research cognizant of the fact that changes in one aspect of social structure necessitate changes elsewhere—changes which in principle, if not yet in fact, are to some degree predictable. We have received, especially from anthropology, weighty indications that the elements of any social system which is cohesive enough to be identified as a whole do not function in isolation, nor can they be changed as discrete units. Thus, the effect of blocking the habitual out-lets for aggression of an aboriginal tribe (e.g., through prohibition of warfare, head-hunting, etc.) does not stop with the elimination of this element. Depending upon other features of the situation, it may result in an increase in witchcraft, in various manifestations of religious cultism, or other changes, each of which may entail secondary adjust-ments. This general statement has been made: "One of the commonest sources of fallacious conclusions lies in the tendency to treat certain aspects of a social structure without taking account of their inter-dependence." [14] Those who use techniques for reducing intergroup hos-tility and have struggled with the phenomena of indirect and boomerang

[14] Talcott Parsons, "Propaganda and Social Control," *Psychiatry,* 5:552 (1942).

reactions to their efforts would probably be the first to see the relevance of this assertion to their daily problems.

The remainder of this chapter deals with a series of empirical propositions concerning intergroup behavior. Each proposition refers to putative facts of actual social life, but no single generalization or hypothesis presented can be taken in isolation from others; nor can these formulations be seen in their proper significance unless viewed in the context of the considerations reviewed in the preceding pages.

Principles, Working Hypotheses, and Assumptions

Most of the propositions about relations among racial, ethnic, and religious groups which are listed hereinafter are current in the literature,[15] although the present wording is usually synthetic rather than drawn from any one source. In some instances in which the hypothesis was not found in explicit form in published material, the present statement represents an inference necessary to "make sense" of actions or statements which have been observed. The total listing may be regarded as a series of notes on problems needing further research. The present formulations can only be tentative and it is certain that they fall far short of exhausting the questions which could be raised, even on the basis of present knowledge. The sole aim of the compilation is to bring together in compact and convenient form a sampling of what is known and surmised in this field. To whatever degree further thinking may be stimulated or research possibilities suggested, the compilation will have served its purpose.

Many, if not most, of the propositions outlined are at present little more than "educated guesses." Certain generalizations, on the other hand, are supported by such a large and consistent body of cumulative observations that their validity under specified conditions is highly probable. Many other generalizations, however, are supported by almost no data other than "expert opinion"; in some instances authorities of equally wide practical experience and scientific knowledge have reached what appear to be diametrically opposite conclusions. There are grounds for suspecting that the seeming disagreement may frequently be traceable to ambiguities in definition and failure to specify the precise conditions

---

[15] Representative sources and quotations are given to illustrate a number of propositions. (Numbers in parentheses refer to items cited in the Selected Bibliography.) However, many of the propositions listed have been put forward in essentially congruent form by many different students of this field. It has not seemed expedient, therefore, to attempt any elaborate or systematic documentation. Incidentally, one of the striking impressions gained from a review of available literature is the existing consensus on a considerable number of basic hypotheses—along with the usually recognized divergences of viewpoint.

within which a given generalization holds true. In other cases it is to be expected that further research will show prevalent hypotheses to be false, or at least in need of reformulation and qualification. In spite of the slight and uncertain factual basis of many of the propositions, it has seemed desirable to outline them as completely and sharply as possible. Nothing is to be gained in the current stage of scientific knowledge in this field from a refusal to formulate hypotheses. In fact, one of the greatest needs appears to be that of making working assumptions explicit and clear, in order to expose significant gaps in knowledge and clarify the specific problems needing research, and also to develop perspective in choosing major emphases and orientations in research.

Although the hypotheses outlined are not all presented as "probably true," they were not selected at random. They were formulated with three criteria in mind: (1) their potential importance for social understanding, policy, and action; (2) their possibilities for fruitful empirical research in the near future; (3) their probable validity. In many instances the criteria were in conflict, as when a proposition of great importance involves such methodological difficulties as to cast doubt on its immediate feasibility as a research hypothesis. Propositions of somewhat dubious validity were included whenever they seemed to hold promise on the basis of one or both of the other criteria. Similarly, some hypotheses of relatively minor social importance were included if they seemed plausible and feasible for research. The propositions are roughly classified under these main headings:

    I. Origins and prevalence of hostility
    II. Types of hostility and conflict
    III. Factors in the incidence of hostility and conflict
    IV. Reactions of minority groups
    V. Approaches for the reduction or control of hostility or conflict.

Since this monograph is specifically oriented to problems of techniques for reducing tension, the inclusion of certain broad propositions which do not directly concern specific techniques deserves comment. It seemed essential to include some of the basic "high order" generalizations to provide a frame of reference for the particularistic propositions. Without some such guiding context the specific assertions might well seem to constitute merely an agglomeration of discrete and unorganized items. On the other hand, any attempt to integrate the materials into a more systematic theoretical scheme seemed premature at this time, although there is a definite possibility that such systematization will be made in the near future.

I. *Origins and Prevalence of Hostility*

1. It is a fact of observation that all individuals brought up in human society manifest some hostility toward other individuals or social groups.

> It would seem a safe estimate that at least four-fifths of the American population lead mental lives in which feelings of group hostility play an appreciable role. (Allport and Kramer, 5, p. 9)

> In every known human society there appears to exist a varying amount of "free-floating aggression." This is thought to be mainly the product of the painful restraints put upon all immature human organisms during the socialization process *and* of the deprivations and frustrations which are incident to adult social life in all societies. (Kluckhohn, 104, p. 224)

> . . . almost every intimate emotional relation between two people which lasts for some time . . . leaves a sediment of feelings of aversion and hostility, which have first to be eliminated by repression. (Freud, 66, p. 34)

2. The amount of hostility at any given time varies greatly among individuals, among specific groups, and among social systems. ("Amount" is defined by observable "manifestations"—ranging from group conflict in a physical sense to the analysis of dreams in personality study.)

3. The amount of hostility varies greatly for given individuals, groups, or social systems at different points in time.

General principle: Hostility is universal, but has a wide range of variation in intensity and incidence.

4. In all known social systems individuals conceive of themselves as belonging to certain groups to which they owe loyalty and within which there is an obligation to repress hostility. Invariably, repressed or suppressed hostilities generated in such we-groups are to some degree directed outside to other groups.

> . . . whatever is different in social custom always arouses attention and tends to set up antagonisms. (K. Young, 220, p. 489)

> The identification of the individual with the group gives the emotional satisfaction of the ego urge, without the pang of conscience which accompanies it apart from the group. (Miller, 145, p. 134)

> The greater and more intense the group feeling, that is, the stronger the identification between members of a group, the greater is the strength of the prejudice against the alien group and against those who are not members of one's own group. (MacCrone, 131, p. 249)

5. Infants and preschool children typically do not exhibit prejudice toward ethnic or racial groups. Prejudice is learned. (Horowitz, 90, and many others)

6. Prejudice may be relatively independent of the direct personal experience of the individual: definite prejudices often exist in the absence of any direct contact with members of the pre-judged group. (*Idem*)

> . . . racial attitudes are not necessarily a function of "contact experience." (Nettler, 155, p. 182)

II. *Types of Hostility and Conflict*

7. Hostility directed outward from the self may operate at three (or more) levels of specificity: (a) generalized, "free-floating" aggression, (b) fixation on specific individuals, (c) fixation on social categories of persons (group hostility).

8. An important factor in racial or ethnic conflict is the pattern of *deflected aggression*. Some of the conditions defining this pattern are:

> (a) Frustrations or deprivations are imposed by sources which are either:
>> (1) difficult to define or locate, or
>> (2) persons or organizations in a position of power or authority over the individual, or
>> (3) persons to whom the individual is closely tied by affectional bonds.
> (b) Aroused hostilities are blocked from direct expression against the sources of frustration.
> (c) Substitute objects of aggression are available and are:
>> (1) highly *visible*, and
>> (2) *vulnerable*, i.e., not in a position to retaliate.
>
> It appears that in the case of direct aggression there is always some displaced aggression accompanying it and adding additional force to the rational attack. (Dollard, 55, p. 19)

This is a widespread, recurrent, and important pattern of emotional structuring in human society and is widely recognized on the level of common-sense observation. Ordinary examples are legion: the child punished by his parents destroys a toy or maltreats his pet; the employee humiliated by his superior "takes it out" on his family; the defeated small businessman joins an anti-minority movement.

III. *Factors in the Incidence of Hostility and Conflict*

Question: What factors are associated with high or low intensity or incidence of hostility?

9. Hostility is a function of *frustration;* under certain conditions, the more frustration of important drives or socially induced needs, the more hostility. (Dollard and others, 56)

10. "Frustration" differs in its effects depending upon whether it is a mere "need-deprivation" or a sensed "personality-threat." (Maslow, 136) Maximum hostility may be expected to result from frustrations which combine these characteristics: (a) they violate normal expectations which are felt to be morally justifiable; (b) they are felt to be unnecessary and avoidable; (c) they are perceived as a threat to the security system of the whole personality. (This usually means, a threat to the individual's sense of status. It is thus quite different from a simple deprivation of a segmental need.)

11. Hostility is a function of "insecurity"; the greater the insecurity, within limits, the more hostility.

> If there be one established generalization from clinical psychology and psychiatry, it is that those who are insecure themselves manifest hostilities toward others. (Kluckhohn, 105, p. 51)

> . . . anxiety is generated by a repressed hostility and . . . it in turn again generates hostility. (Horney, 89, p. 89)

12. Whatever its sources, hostility does not automatically lead to interpersonal or intergroup conflict. Instead, it may be structured in a variety of ways which, however, are not indeterminate but are the outcomes of specific types of social situations.

13. Once generated, hostility is structured intrapersonally through such familiar psychological mechanisms as repression, projection, and displacement.

> Aggression, whether overt or masked, is not, to be sure, the only possible adjustive response. Withdrawal, passivity, sublimation, conciliation, flight and other responses are sometimes effective in reducing the motivation of those who have been deprived or threatened. (Kluckhohn, 105, p. 51)

14. The amount or frequency of interpersonal or intergroup overt aggression varies inversely with the strength of the anticipatory responses regarding punishment.

Assumption: There is usually greater anticipation of punishment for overt than for non-overt aggression or substitute responses. (Doob and Sears, 57)

15. The overtness of aggression varies positively with the strength of instigation to a frustrated goal-response.

Assumption: Overt aggression is more satisfying to the individual than non-overt aggression. (*Ibid.*)

16. The frequency of substitute responses varies positively with the strength of anticipatory responses to punishment-for-being-aggressive. (*Ibid.*)

17. The frequency of substitute responses varies inversely with the strength of instigation to a frustrated goal-response.

Assumption: Direct aggression is more satisfying to the individual than indirect or displaced overt aggression. (*Ibid.*)

18. Whether hostility becomes focused upon *groups* is *in part* determined by:

    (a) *Visibility* of groups
        (1) Physical appearance: color, physiognomy, dress, etc.
        (2) Social definition (including "propaganda" emphasizing differences)
    (b) *Contact* of groups
    (c) *Competition* of groups
    (d) Differences in *values* and behavior patterns considered as expressing values (language, sex mores, manners, personal aggressiveness, etc.)

19. Minimum conditions for conflict include (a) contact, (b) visibility, and (c) competition. (Reductions in the values of these variables will, in certain combinations, reduce the probability of conflict. Under some circumstances conflict seems to be facilitated by minimal "impersonal" contact, inhibited by close "personal" contact.)

20. Where a basis for social categorization exists, that is, in group relations, some degree of prejudice-hostility always appears when there is the combination of *visibility* and *competition*. (It does not necessarily follow that the degree of hostility bears a linear relation to the other variables. For example, it has been suggested that hostility is especially likely when a competing group is just noticeably different.)

> Economic factors, if they are to have any effect upon group prejudice, must presuppose the existence of the psychologically prior division into an in-and-out group. It is not because of their economic competition that Jews and Japanese excite hostility, but it is because they are Jews or Japanese that their competition is [regarded as] unfair, or underhand, or an offense to those who are neither Jews nor Japanese. (MacCrone, 131, p. 254)
>
> *Group antagonisms seem to be inevitable when two peoples in contact with each other may be distinguished by differentiating*

characteristics, either inborn or cultural, and are actual or potential competitors. Only by eliminating the outward evidences of distinction, such as color, dress, or language, or by removing the competitive factor, may racial antagonisms be destroyed. (D. Young, 216, p. 586)

The tension level of any social grouping is in part a function of the relative emphasis in that group's culture upon *participation in common values* as over against individual or group *acquisition of scarce "goods."*

In every social system people act in orientation to certain values which can be shared by everyone, and which are not scarce in the sense that one individual's sharing will reduce others' enjoyment of the value. The most ready and conspicuous examples are religious salvation, and group (e.g., national) prestige. All adherents to a religious faith can participate in its values—all, for example, can have salvation—without any member's "success" detracting from that of any other member. Similarly, in this respect, all Americans are presumed to share in any increase or decrease in the prestige of the nation considered as a collectivity. National prestige as such is "participated in" rather than "divided up." On the other hand, in every social system people also act in orientation to scarce, divisible, and divisive values. This is, of course, true even of those who share a common culture in such other respects as language, religion, family mores, political ideology, and so on. The main classes of scarce, divisible values are: wealth, power, and prestige within a given group or culture. In any given state of the economy, the more economic goods held or consumed by one individual, the less there are for others.[16] Power consists of control over others; hence it·is inherently scarce and distributive. Prestige status is meaningful only in terms of relative ranking within a system: for one individual or group to be "high" requires that others be ranked "lower."

Thus every society has to work out some equilibrium of relative emphasis upon these two broad classes of action orientation. It seems to be generally agreed among serious students of American society that our culture places a rather extraordinary stress upon competition for distributive values. The "competitive" motif is not merely a matter of such competition being permitted; rather, the striving for "success" is

[16] That is, abstracting from the complex interlocking of economic interests in a dynamic process through time. The fact that the long-run economic interests of immediately competing individuals or groups may be harmonious is, in this context, irrelevant to the fact that at a given time there is only a limited quantity of utilities available for distribution. The division of utilities, which by definition are scarce relative to the desires for them, is that of the allocation of goods in the short run, regardless of ultimate congruities or clashes of interest.

positively enjoined to such an extent that in many areas and classes it approaches the status of a culturally obligatory pattern. At the same time, American society—at least in comparison with many older, more stable, more homogeneous societies—appears historically to have a relatively low development of the shared, nondivisible values.[17] These two aspects seem clearly interrelated. Thus insofar as emphasis upon religious, other-worldly values has declined, this must in itself reinforce tendencies for "worldly" competition, other things being at all equal.

The competition which is significant for the analysis of group hostility is not just any kind of competition but that which revolves around basic security in subsistence and status. In this connection the importance of status-mobility in the United States is difficult to overstress. Rising and falling on the status-prestige scale is nominally free, and in actuality has been very widespread, i.e., the dominant institutional pattern has been that of achieved rather than ascribed status. In fact, "intensive competition" and "emphasis upon achieved status" are merely two formulations of the same situation. As Charles Horton Cooley pointed out, there are only two polar systems for ranking individuals in the social order: either inherited status or some form of competition.[18]

Note:

In the following propositions the condition "all other things being equal" should be understood in each case. Since "other conditions" are rarely "equal," this is a rigorous limitation on concrete generalizations.

21. The greater the differentiation of groups and of individual social roles in a society, the greater the probabilities of group conflict.

> We are living in a more complex and developed culture than any before, and the possibilities of confusion and conflict are correspondingly the greatest. (Pettee, 162, p. xii)

> In complex civilization, therefore, group antagonism necessarily increases because every differentiation (division of labor, heterogeneity) brings about particularistic interests. (Alexander, 1, p. 28)

22. Intergroup conflict is the more likely the more rapid and far-reaching the social changes to which individuals have to adjust.

[17] This situation is certainly complex, and there are some evidences that nationalistic feeling and the values of the "American Creed" are of more importance in national integration than is commonly supposed.
[18] "Personal Competition," Chapter IV in his *Sociological Theory and Social Research* (New York: Henry Holt and Company, 1930). Cf. especially pp. 163–175.

Theorem 1: A people forced to make readjustments are likely to display increased energies of hostilities in some direction, even when their "objective" situation is more favorable than in the status quo ante period. This prediction is particularly indicated when the people have been deprived of habitual outlets for aggression. (Kluckhohn, 104, p. 226)

23. Open conflict is the more likely the more *direct* the intergroup competition for the distributive rewards of wealth, power, prestige, or other scarce values, and the more *successful* the competition of vulnerable groups.

When there is an actual threat to the dominance of the in-group, socially legitimated hostilities may appear. (Dollard, 55, pp. 19–20)

24. Intergroup hostility and conflict are the more likely the greater the general level of tension in the society as a result of economic depression, prior cultural conflict, or various types of social disorganization.

. . . the most important source of virulent anti-Semitism is probably the projection on the Jew, as a symbol, of free-floating aggression, springing from insecurities and social disorganization. (Parsons, 160, p. 121)

Throughout the history of the United States there seems to have been a direct correlation between the peaks of nativist spirit and the valleys of exceptional economic difficulty. (D. Young, 217, p. 133)

25. Disruption of stable expectations of interpersonal conduct tends to be productive of intergroup conflict. Insofar as institutional patterning of behavior breaks down in important life-areas, predictability is lowered, with a consequent increase in anxiety and in various types of frustration. Free-floating aggression thus produced easily becomes focused on ethnic, racial, or religious groups. (The special conditions conducive to this focus are outlined in other propositions: cf. 8, 18, 19, 20.)

26. The intensity of intergroup hostility varies inversely with the number and adequacy of "harmless" outlets for aggression within a society. (What are "harmless outlets" is a matter of valuation from other points of view. One possible definition is: those avenues for discharge of aggressive impulses which do not violate major norms necessary for the structural continuity of the social system. These in our society might include competitive sports, swearing, some forms of aggressive interpersonal joking, certain uses of alcohol, drama and pageantry, etc.)

27. Migration of a visibly different group into a given area increases

the likelihood of conflict; the probability of conflict is the greater (a) the larger the ratio of the incoming minority to the resident population, and (b) the more rapid the influx.

28. Conflict is especially likely in periods of rapid change in levels of living. The probability of conflict is increased insofar as the changes have a differential impact on various groups.

29. Hostilities and conflicts among ethnic or racial groups are to an appreciable extent interchangeable with "class" conflicts. (This hypothesis states that ethnic conflicts may prevent focalization of class conflicts, e.g., labor vs. employers, and that interclass struggle may direct a given "charge" of hostility away from ethnic targets.)

30. Given a social group which is "a going concern," a sensed outside threat *to the group as a whole* will result in heightened internal cohesion and an increased centralization of control within the group.

This appears to be one of the most important general principles of group dynamics. It is applicable to a large number of concrete events, ranging from nations at war to the behavior of neighborhood factions, and it is supported by a wealth of observation. However, it holds true only under very specific conditions: (a) The group must be a "going concern," i.e., there must be a minimal consensus among the constituent individuals that the aggregate is a group, and that its preservation as an entity is worth while. The case of France in 1940 may be taken, in part, as illustrative of the consequence of inadequate collective consensus. (b) There must be recognition of an outside threat which is thought to menace the group as a whole, not just some parts of it. An objective threat is not causal, in this respect, unless recognized. On the other hand, external groups may be defined as threatening in the absence of objective danger.

31. The probability of internal group conflict is lowered by the presence of an outside threat which endangers all groups.

> Hatred of a common enemy is the most powerful known agency for producing group unity. (Edwards, 59, p. 55)

> Groups which arise out of conflict tend to disintegrate when opposition ceases. (Hiller, 87, p. 30)

> The best safeguard against internal disruptive antagonisms seems to be the presence of an external enemy which gives the hostile impulses an external target. (Alexander, 1, p. 28)

To find a common dislike is apparently one of the most frequent and gratifying experiences in creating a bond between individuals. It is as though uncomfortable latent hostilities between the two parties are removed by deflection to a third, outside object.

32. Focalization of hostility upon a given group is probably inhibited by a multiplicity of vulnerable minorities in the society; a society riven by many minor cleavages is in less danger of open mass conflict than a society with only one or a few cleavages. (However, there is a possibility that a socially incapacitating chaos of group antagonisms may generate a demand for unification which will involve focusing hostility upon a selected minority.)

In the most extreme case of mass violence:

> An essential step in the development of revolution is the gradual concentration of public dissatisfaction upon some one institution and the persons representing it . . . In the earlier stages . . . the dissatisfaction is diffused and dissipated. (Edwards, 59, p. 46)

33. Among the members of any dominant group the greatest incidence of open conflict behavior toward a given minority will be found among those classes which are most vulnerable to competition from the minority. It is a legitimate guess from the scattered evidence at hand that group conflict is not so much a correlate of *differences* in status as it is of *changes* in status and in the highly visible symbols thereof.

> Aggressive responses are apparently powerfully excited by fear. (Dollard, 55, p. 18)

34. Group conflict arises in part because it satisfies certain individual or group needs. Unless these needs can be eliminated or greatly diminished or satisfied through other means, there will remain a possibility of conflict, no matter how skillfully formal techniques of diversion and control are applied.

> What seems to be required first is an analysis of the prejudiced individual to find out not where he acquired the prejudice but *why he needs it.* (Watson, 210, p. 181)

35. Maintenance of the "American Creed" in intergroup matters is usually strongest among small groups of professional and upper class persons, and emphasis upon its univeral values circulates downward in the social stratification pyramid. In general, only persons in "upper" groups have sufficient security to work actively for innovations in the direction of greater privileges for minorities. Although behavior in nondiscriminatory labor unions and certain related organizations may appear to contradict this hypothesis, it may be argued that even in such cases

the impetus toward nondiscrimination tends in the main to come from the top organizational levels. (Suggested by Charles Dollard)

36. Historically viewed, American lower class groups have always had successive groups of recent immigrants which provided both a basis for compensatory feelings of superiority and a target for release of structurally determined frustrations. Each level in the class structure could thus control and subdue those still lower by displacing its aggression on lower groups as a means of maintaining its own sense of status.

The cessation of large-scale immigration has thus removed an important element of flexibility in the balancing system for controlling intergroup hostilities.

37. In American society psychological insecurity concerning position on the scale of social stratification is most intense in the lower middle class. This class may, therefore, be expected to exhibit a maximum of free-floating hostility.

38. An important element of the American value-system is the belief that individuals have an obligation to accept the results of fair competition i.e., to be a "good loser." Hence competition tends to turn into conflict whenever doubts are raised concerning the fairness of the competition or the validity of the rules of the game.

Experience seems to show that American groups do not easily accept the results of competition or other processes which appear to them to be responsible for catastrophic declines in their social position.

39. Conflict between persons of different identifiable groups is the more likely when there is no clear definition of the situation, especially with regard to detailed patterns of "appropriate" personal behavior.

> . . . the intensity of intergroup antagonism varies with the frequency of contacts between minority and majority individuals not in accord with customary practice under an accepted social definition of status relationship. (D. Young, 217, pp. 65–66)

40. Mass violence (e.g., race riots) is most likely under the following conditions: (a) prolonged frustration, leading to a high tension level; (b) presence of population elements with a propensity to violence (especially lower class, adolescent males in socially disorganized areas); (c) a highly visible and rapid change in intergroup relations; (d) a precipitating incident of intergroup conflict.

IV. *Reactions of Minority Groups*

41. Marked self-consciousness and sensitivity is characteristic of those minority group members occupying ambiguous social positions in modern America.

42. Militancy, except for sporadic and short-lived uprisings, is not characteristic of the most deprived and oppressed groups, but rather of those who have gained considerable rights so that they are able realistically to hope for more.

> The consciousness of repression leads to discontent only when it is felt unnecessary. This is the reason why a rising class, which is actually becoming constantly better off objectively, generally rebels most readily, and why the most severe repression has so often failed to cause a revolution. (Pettee, 162, p. 32)

43. A militant reaction from a minority group is most likely when (a) the group's position is rapidly improving, or (b) when it is rapidly deteriorating, especially if this follows a period of improvement.

> The whole argument about distress and expansive ambition as causes of revolution [conflict] may be resolved if one remembers that a shoe may pinch, either because the foot has grown, or because the shoe has shrunken. (*Ibid.*, p. 15)

44. Prejudice against Negroes and certain other minorities is likely to be especially vigorous and vocal among ethnic groups which have been only recently "Americanized" and which are attempting to move up in the class hierarchy. (This tendency is intensified by any discrepancy between the ideology of upward social mobility and actual rigidities in the social structure.)

45. Mutual hostilities sometimes arise between minority groups which are themselves the object of aggression by the dominant majority, e.g., anti-Semitism among Negroes. In other instances minorities combine in mutual support against prejudice and discrimination on the part of the majority groups. The conditions determining these opposite types of behavior are not well understood.

V. *Approaches for the Reduction or Control of Hostility and Conflict*

(A) *General Orientation*

46. The two extreme "solutions" for eliminating a given group conflict are: (a) complete insulation, e.g., geographic exclusion, and (b) complete assimilation.

47. The main theoretical possibilities for minimizing a given group conflict are:

- (a) actual reduction in hostility
- (b) no change in hostility level, but a rechannelization to substitute targets (in the extreme case, diffusion to a variety of objects)

(c) no change in hostility level and retention of major object-fixation, but repression of overt conflict.

48. The reduction of intergroup conflict depends upon:

(a) reduction of hostility, which depends upon minimization of frustrations and insecurities and their attendant anxieties
(b) proper canalization of existing hostilities, through sanctions, diversions, redefinition of situations, etc.

Thus the anxiety and frustration which our social order continually generates can be reduced to manageable proportions only if at least two conditions are fulfilled: First, if our physical and economic situations are reasonably comfortable and secure, and, secondly if we derive adequate security and gratification from satisfactory inter-personal relationships. If people are anxious and frustrated by society and if, moreover, they live in social isolation . . . many of them will try to discharge their aggressions explosively through acts of violence. (Bettelheim, 6, p. 36)

In attacking many specific phenomena of social pathology one is attacking "symptoms"—not "causes." The result, if successful at all, will be merely to shift the currents of hostility—not to eliminate them. An attack upon "causes" must consist: (a) in ameliorating basic situations which are productive of "realistic" worries and hostilities; (b) in devising improved techniques of child socialization and of subsequent inter-personal relations so that the total amount of "free-floating aggression" is decreased. (Kluckhohn, 104, p. 238)

49. An individual does not act only in *more* or *less* prejudiced ways: he acts in *different* ways depending upon the function of the basic value structure in his personality in action.

The findings . . . are clear proof that prejudiced responses are not dissociated from the total pattern of personal life . . . Those who have a jungle philosophy of life (viewing the world as basically evil and dangerous) are generally prejudiced. (Allport and Kramer, 5, pp. 34, 38)

50. Any given pattern of intergroup hostility and conflict varies in its intensity and in its implications depending upon whether it is (a) traditional and sanctioned as a "legitimate" channel for aggression-release, or (b) in opposition to nominally dominant value-patterns.

The most intense conflicts, such as those which merge into mass political actions, are to be expected when: (1) situation *a* co-exists with an increased threat to the dominant group, or (2) situation *b* has moved close to widespread repudiation of the dominant values.

51. Simultaneous direct attack on every form of intergroup discrimination is likely to intensify the reaction it attempts to stop. Programs aimed against discrimination will be least likely to set off unmanageable "nativistic" reactions by proceeding one point at a time, and by starting with items of lowest negative symbolic potential.

> Generally speaking, any policy which tends to make Jews as Jews more conspicuous, and particularly those Jews who are at the same time vulnerable symbols in other respects, would tend to be an invitation to anti-Semitic reaction. Thus, indiscriminate attack on every form of existent discrimination, regardless of anything but the immediate effectiveness of the means, is not likely to achieve the actual elimination of anti-Semitism, but on the contrary to intensify the reactions it attempts to stop. (Parsons, 160, p. 121)

52. A general principle of approach is that, except in acute crisis situations, problems of group conflict are usually most readily resolved by indirection rather than by frontal assault. In propaganda, for example, direct arguments tend to present a sharp issue which arouses maximum resistance; a more effective procedure is to emphasize common aims and suggest group integration as a means for their attainment.

Insofar as possible, if it is desired to avoid defensive hostility, guided changes in intergroup relations must be made in such a way as to avoid or minimize the interpretation that they threaten security with regard to those things in which the groups have important emotional commitments. (It should be clear, however, that various gradualistic ameliorative proposals for reducing hostility or conflict do not directly reach the problem of "interested," calculated discrimination or the conscious use of group visibility as a means for perpetuating a privileged social and economic position.)

53. Where strong prejudice is present in a group which is highly self-conscious, and strongly bound together, outside criticism of its prejudice is likely to be taken as an attack on the group; and *one* immediate effect is to strengthen the prejudice, which by virtue of the attack becomes a symbol of in-group membership and solidarity. (Two historical cases are especially good illustrations: Northern criticism of race relations in the Southern states; outside criticism of the Afrikaans-speaking whites in the Union of South Africa.)

(B) *Information and Education*

54. The likelihood of conflict is reduced by education and propaganda emphases upon characteristics and values *common* to various groups rather than upon intergroup *differences*. (But there is danger that attitudes thus created may lead to expectation of greater similarity than later experience demonstrates, and this can lead to disillusionment and secondary reinforcement of hostility. A second qualification is that some persons holding to a doctrine of cultural pluralism advocate awareness of differences on the assumption that acceptance of differences comes only after a transitional period, which may involve temporary intensification of hostility.)

55. Favorable attitudes and the extent of information about given groups are positively, but slightly, correlated; effects are not clearly proven in detail but the general evidence is positive.

> Altogether, our rather meager evidence suggests that those who know most about other races and peoples tend to have favorable attitudes about them, particularly in the case of those more frequently met, such as Negroes in this country. (Murphy, Murphy and Newcomb, 152, p. 1001)

56. The effects of imparting a given type of information about minority groups—under given circumstances—differ, depending upon the extent and degree to which the recipients already have favorable or unfavorable attitudes toward the group or groups in question.

> . . . the influence of information upon attitude may vary with the nature of that attitude. (Nettler, 155, p. 182)

Related sub-hypotheses:

(a) "Information is more effective as an attitude determinant where the attitudinal norm [in a given group] is unfavorable." (*Ibid.,* p. 185)

(b) Imparting of information will have greater positive effects upon individuals who stand in an intermediate attitudinal position than upon those at either extreme.

(c) Imparting information to the more militant of those prejudiced against the group will rarely produce an immediate change in attitudes and may intensify hostile reactions: a nonlogical prejudice may be transformed into consciously irrational hostility.

57. The mere giving of objective general information in print or by lecture about a group which is the object of hostility has only a slight

effect, or no effect, in reducing hostility—at least in the short run. (This is the negative statement of the hypothesis that the communication of scientific information or other factual data tends to undermine the strength of prejudice. Any research on this point must be careful to specify the content and the conditions of communication, to distinguish between short-run and long-run effects, and to watch for differences between effects on isolated individuals or small groups and effect on communities as wholes.)

> . . . straight lectures on the interests, rights, and virtues of minority groups accomplish very little. (Allport, 2, p. 6)

58. Even with a uniform body of instructional materials about a given group or groups, the effects of instruction upon recipients will vary appreciably with the basic attitudes and "personality" of the instructor.

59. Insofar as education or propaganda reduces hostility toward any specific group or toward out-groups in general, it does so largely by rechannelizing aggressive impulses rather than removing them.

60. Attempts to reduce intergroup hostility by education will be the more effective, (a) the more the learners are convinced in the beginning that they themselves are not under attack for their opinions; and (b) the more the learners are allowed initially to express freely their verbal hostilities to instructors who maintain an atmosphere of calm objectivity.

> It is an axiom that people cannot be taught who feel that they are at the same time being attacked. It is also an axiom that they learn very little unless they want to learn. (Allport, 2, p. 5)

> . . . re-trainers who encounter more resistance than they expect may need to provide more abundantly than they do for the free expression of hostility. (*Ibid.*, p. 9)

61. Educational programs will have maximum effects, all other things being equal, when information is presented as part of the ordinary action of a group in carrying out its usual social function (e.g., as part of general teacher training, job training for public officials, conferences of industrialists, labor leaders, merchants, real estate dealers, etc.).

62. Prejudices are most likely to be changed by the imparting of information about the object of prejudice when the learners themselves actively participate in gathering the relevant information.

> . . . complete acceptance of previously rejected facts can be achieved best through the discovery of these facts by the group members themselves. (Lewin and Grabbe, 121, p. 63)

63. Changing the attitudes of *groups* rather than isolated individuals is the more effective approach for breaking up intergroup stereotypes and prejudices.

> . . . many stereotypes and dislikes are anchored not so much in the individual's personality as in the face-to-face groups to which the individual belongs and which determine his standards and ideals. (Lewin, 120, p. 186)

> The group is more resistant to environmental change than is the individual . . . The impact of cultural differences or of social disapproval is weakened by the presence of others who share it. (Strother, 196, p. 51)

> Permanent belongingness in an organized locally rooted, solidary social system is the only concrete matrix capable of grasping and involving the whole motivation of man . . . Consequently, this sort of matrix is ultimately the most effective setting for the re-educational process. (Bales, 11, p. 21)

64. Hostility is decreased by any activity which leads members of conflicting groups to identify their own values and life-activities in individuals of the other group. To be most effective this requires devices for inducing *personal* identification before the introduction of group labels.

Dictum: Personalize, personalize, personalize.

(C) *Direct Reorientation of Values*

65. In intergroup relations, as in many others, word-of-mouth propaganda, especially that which appears spontaneous and informal, is more effective than visual or formal propaganda in influencing attitudes and behavior.

So far as specific media are concerned, the scanty evidence suggests this general order of effectiveness: (1) direct personal communication (speeches, lectures, etc.); (2) radio; (3) printed materials. However, the research results also suggest that the order of effectiveness varies with the subject matter, the type of appeal, and the type of audience.

66. In intergroup relations, as in many others, propaganda which makes an "emotional" (value-oriented) appeal is likely to be more effective than that which is restricted to factual appeal.

But this plausible assertion may be countered with the view that such appeals arouse relatively uncontrolled emotions which are not likely to lead to tolerant or humane behavior. It certainly appears that there are sufficient dangers in strongly emotional propaganda to warrant careful testing with different types of audiences.

67. In intergroup relations, as in many others, the "propaganda of the deed" is especially likely to have effects upon attitudes and behavior.

68. Propaganda which appeals for minority rights on the basis of the group's achievements tends beyond a certain point to arouse insecurity-hostility in the dominant group by stressing group differences and competitive success.

This hypothesis implies that appeals which suggest a status-threat to prejudiced groups are to be avoided.

69. It is dangerous technique to employ *mass* propaganda emphasizing "rising tides of prejudice" as a means intended to mobilize defenders of minority rights and good intergroup relations. Such propaganda is likely to have a boomerang effect upon slightly prejudiced or wavering elements: it creates the presumption of group support for hostile actions.

70. Appeals to conscience or ethics must be carefully handled, if they are to diminish rather than intensify hostility. In general, such appeals are probably most effective in reinforcing the sentiments of persons who are already convinced; they are probably not effective (immediately, at least) with militant anti-ethnics, and may even result in increased hostility as a reaction to guilt-feelings. That is, where individuals are utilizing prejudice to satisfy strong emotional urges, activation of the conscience-functions may tend to heighten psychological conflict and thus to result in increasingly devious or irrational hostilities.

71. Appeals to local pride are sometimes useful in motivating leaders to prevent open conflict. Mass violence is widely regarded in America as bringing discredit upon the community in which it occurs.

72. Conflict is discouraged by providing, through sources of high general prestige, for specific public commendation of individuals of the dominant group who work for toleration, minority rights, mutual understanding, and the like.

73. An effective propaganda approach in intergroup relations is that which emphasizes national symbols and common American achievements, sacrifices, destinies, etc., while unobtrusively indicating the common participation of minority group members.

74. Other things being equal, the blocking of hostile impulses and their deflection into harmless channels is facilitated by any devices which strongly remind individuals of commonly acknowledged cultural pre-

scriptions against hostility to other groups. Examples of such devices are:
(a) pronouncements by representatives of moral and political authority;
(b) dramatic ceremonial affirmation of the relevant patterns and values;
(c) public reward and (sometimes) punishment.

75. Conflict and hostility are rendered less probable by any activity which leads individuals to *take for granted* the other group (e.g., moving pictures which show Negroes as members of various kinds of groups, where the emphasis of presentation is upon what the group is doing).

76. Individuals who have been exposed to strongly religious training, or who participate in organized religious activities, do not necessarily manifest less hostility or greater tolerance than individuals not having these characteristics. Only certain types of religious training are effective in lessening intergroup hostility.

> Religious training in itself does *not* lessen prejudice. But religious training which successfully stresses tolerance and brotherhood *does* tend to lessen prejudice. (Allport and Kramer, 5, p. 38)

Note: Certain studies have shown a correlation "cluster" consisting of attitudes of nationalism, out-group prejudices, conventional and rigid moral codes, and religiosity (study of Frenkel-Brunswik and Sanford; an unpublished study by Louis Guttman indicates a correlation between prejudice and conventional religiosity).

77. The effects of public refutation of hostile rumors vary with the nature of the refutation and with the type of rumor and attendant situation, e.g.:

(a) *In chronic but relatively stable and mild intergroup tensions,* rumors are probably best ignored, or refuted only by indirection and propaganda of the deed.

(b) *Rumors of unusual character, intensity, or prevalence* (e.g., role of minorities in the armed forces in war) probably should be met by "official" propaganda. However, publicizing the rumors themselves should be avoided; the refutation should be as indirect (nonmanifest) as is consistent with the necessity of gaining attention.

(c) *In crisis situations* (pre-riot, etc.) refutation of rumors of hostile intentions or of hostile actions of opposing groups, weakness of control forces, and the like tends to check conflict.

Note: Contrary assumptions are also advanced by experienced authorities. Almost nothing is definitely established on these propositions.

(D) *Intergroup Contact and Collaboration*

78. Lessened hostility will result from arranging intergroup collaboration, on the basis of personal association of individuals as functional equals, on a common task jointly accepted as worth while.

> To achieve any kind of mutual understanding and regard, people must share experiences which permit the interplay of character and personality. They must share a common objective. (Lett, 115, p. 35)

> . . . where peoples of various cultures and races freely and genuinely associate, there tensions and difficulties, prejudices and confusions, dissolve; where they do not associate, where they are isolated from one another, there prejudice and conflict grow like a disease. (Brameld, 24, p. 245)

79. (a) Personal contacts between members of different groups are generally most effective in producing friendly relations when the individuals are of the same, or nearly the same, economic and social status and share similar interests and tastes.

> The interracial agencies have the theory that prejudice is broken down more easily and understanding built up more rapidly through the personal contact of the races than by any other method . . . An effort is made to bring together people of the same age and cultural level, following the belief that groups which have many things in common will achieve a better understanding. (Baker, 10, p. 178)

> Conversely, contact between members of groups holding very different economic and social status (or between members of groups equally deprived of status, e.g., the poor whites and poor blacks) intensifies rivalry and the desire to establish status at the expense of one another. (Allport and Kramer, 5, p. 23)

(b) But these statements can be matched with different opinions:

> The contact of the races in America when it is on the basis of equality often breeds suspicion, fear, resentment, disturbance, and at times open conflict. As long as the contact is on "the superior and inferior" relation, the two groups can mingle on a social and intimate basis without friction. (Baker, 10, p. 120)

> Yet racial attitudes and stereotypes do change. They change, however, not because of exceptional and intimate understanding friendships between individuals of antagonistic groups, but when the basic conditions which have produced group hatreds are removed. (D. Young, 216, p. 14)

> Closeness of contact, or familiarity as such, between groups will not necessarily lead to a reduction in social distance between the individual members, unless it is accompanied by the discovery that there are elements shared in common. Otherwise such familiarity, by enhancing the differences that divide the two groups, will only lead to an increase in social distance. (MacCrone, 131, p. 178)

(c) Evidently research testing of sharply defined hypotheses is especially appropriate with regard to intergroup contacts. The great importance attached to the subject by action agencies is coexistent with a wide variety of opinions among persons with long experience and study in the field. The differing results of intergroup contacts at various times and places, and the divergent assumptions and hypotheses drawn from these experiences, strongly suggest a need for further definition, isolation, and control of potentially important variables in contact-experiences. A few tentative suggestions as to such variables are given below.

(d) In personal contacts between members of different racial, ethnic, or religious groups, the effects upon the prejudice-hostility level will be contingent in part upon some or all of the following variables:

(1) The general status of the minority group in relation to the majority groups. E.g., the fact that Jewish persons tend to occupy higher occupational positions than Negroes will influence the results of specific types of contacts.

(2) The class positions of the various individuals within their own group, and the comparative status of individuals in the one group relative to the other

(3) The initial prejudice-hostility level of the individuals involved

(4) The character and extent of prejudice in the total social milieu within which the contacts occur. E.g., the effects of Negro-white contacts in Mississippi may be expected to differ from those occuring in Maine.

(5) The actual and anticipated duration of contact

(6) The "intimacy" of contact (actual and anticipated)

(7) The extent to which contact is explicitly defined in terms of intergroup relations, or only with reference to other activities of common interest

(8) The strength of competitive and noncompetitive factors in relations between members of the two groups

(9) Number of persons involved

(10) The degree to which the situation of contact is defined as "real," that is, the extent to which the participants expect it to affect their personal relations within their accustomed group

associations. This would be important, for example, in differential reactions to a mixed tour in a foreign country as against associations of equal intimacy in the individuals' own local community.

(e) *Illustrative qualifying hypotheses:*

(1) In the case of Negroes and probably Spanish Americans and other "depressed" groups majority members may be most favorably affected by contacts with persons of equal or higher status.

(2) In the case of Jews Gentiles may be most favorably affected by contacts with those of the same or lower status.

(3) In both (1) and (2) the effects will vary with the class position of the majority group member in his own group.

(4) In all cases the effects will vary with the anticipated duration of the contacts and with their anticipated effects upon the individual's social relations within his own group.

80. Personal association of members of different groups is most effective in reducing hostility and increasing understanding when the focus of interaction is upon a common interest, goal, or task rather than upon intergroup association as such. (The converse hypothesis, that such association should explicitly stress the purpose of promoting group understanding, is often acted upon.)

81. Increased concrete knowledge of the life of a minority group, especially of particular persons whose behavior does not fit stereotyped conceptions, tends to break up rigid stereotypes and under some conditions to diffuse or decrease hostility.

82. Prejudice is reduced by arranging for personal, intimate contacts of members of different groups who share important tastes and interests in common. (Prejudice is usually only increased by casual, public contacts, especially in urban situations.) Contact must be intensive enough to result in personal likes *and* dislikes which help to break up stereotypes. It is not wise policy for a minority to insist upon wholesale liking of its members to the point of claiming "discrimination" unless universal acceptability is granted the group.

> . . . a person may have prejudices which stand in direct opposition to his personal experience. . . . favorable experiences with members of another group, even if they are frequent, do not necessarily diminish prejudices toward that group . . . only when the individuals can be perceived as "typical representatives" of that group,

is the experience with individuals likely to affect the stereotype. (Lewin and Grabbe, 121, p. 58)

A factor of great importance in bringing about a change in sentiment is the degree to which the individual becomes actively involved in the problem. (*Ibid.*, p. 59)

83. Diminution of hostility may be expected when it is possible to arrange for ritualized conflict or competition between groups which cut across ethnic or racial lines (e.g., a local athletic team which includes an "ethnic" playing against a rival team which is also multi-ethnic).

84. Hostility is reduced by arranging for reverse role-taking in public drama or ceremony (e.g., an anti-Negro person plays a realistic Negro role). Re-training in intergroup relations among highly prejudiced persons is facilitated by arranging "rehearsal" situations in which initial contacts with out-group members may be made without the feeling of "playing for keeps." To change permanently and to stabilize behavior patterns, however, the "players" must be led through increasingly realistic participations.

85. Participation in public rituals and ceremonies re-affirming solidarity and pledging cooperation works toward inhibition of tendencies for intergroup conflict.

The same hypothesis holds true for joint participation in common rituals, festivals, and ceremonies (e.g., joint Christmas-Chanukah observances, patriotic observances).

86. Formation of committees of mixed membership to deal with local problems tends to reduce the likelihood of conflict for the time being. But:

. . . minority groups . . . wonder, publicly, whether some of these committees may not be doing more to inhibit than to stimulate action. (Liveright, 127, p. 106)

. . . many committees on minority problems do not see their way clear for action and that frustration may lead to dangerous disillusionment. (Lewin, 120, p. 188)

87. In any integration of minority members into a work situation *on the initiative of higher control-groups in an organization,* acceptance is facilitated by arranging for representation of the minority in the upper as well as the lower levels of the organization. This arrangement is

necessary to forestall accusations that workers are forced to accept that which the control-group itself will not tolerate.

> The smart personnel man will always start his nondiscrimination program with employment of a Negro or Negress in his own department or on the top management level. (Haas and Fleming, 79, p. 55)

88. *Problem:* The introduction of minority group members into new areas or activities may be accomplished by: (a) gradual introduction of selected individuals, with a minimum of prior discussion or announcement; (b) statement that the minority will be introduced, accompanied by a considerable volume of information, exhortation, and discussion prior to the change itself; (c) polling, or otherwise determining wishes of the majority group, in advance of the change—the results being understood to constitute a binding decision. (This may be done either with or without an information and discussion program.)

Examples:
>   (1) . . . discrepancy between the imagined problems and the actual problems is so great as to lead some administrators to question whether advance discussion may not discourage steps which could have been taken if the matter had not become controversial before it had been tried. (Watson, 210, p. 178)
>   (2) Haas and Fleming (79, pp. 52–53) recommend this procedure. In essentials it was used by the National Smelting Company (reported by Rubin and Segal, 181).
>   (3) A department store polled white employees and found them opposed to the entrance of Negro employees, thus blocking further immediate action (reported by Watson, 210, p. 178).

Hypotheses:
>   (1) Procedure *a* will be most effective, in securing acceptance with a minimum of conflict, in cases in which there are relatively tolerant initial attitudes in the majority population.
>   (2) Procedure *b* will be the more effective method in the case of populations having relatively strong initial prejudice.
>   (3) Procedure *c* will almost always be the least effective of the three methods named.

(E) *Legislation and Law Enforcement*

89. The existence of laws protecting the rights of minorities and court decisions upholding these laws tend, in the long run, to decrease con

flict over the rights involved. This result appears because of at least the following factors: (a) the set toward generalized conformity resulting from the typical training of individuals in any social system; (b) insofar as effective sanctions are actually invoked, some deterrent effect is possible and, more important, those who apply or acquiesce in the application of sanctions thereby reinforce their own sentiments toward conformity; (c) the presumption of legitimacy discourages conflict over rights claimed by minorities, by mobilizing intrapersonality "conscience" functions of majority-group members.

90. Whenever there is sufficient flexibility in public attitudes, the abolition of legal discriminations and disabilities in the long run will reduce hostility and conflict.

> In opposition to a common belief, school segregation tends to increase rather than prevent race conflicts. (D. Young, 216, p. 495)

91. A general expectation of authoritative intervention and the possibility of punishment for acts of violence, whether in group conflict or in individual incidents, will decrease the probability of open conflict.

> (a) Tendencies toward open conflict are inhibited by the publicized presence of effective, well disciplined, and impartial law-enforcement agencies.
> (b) Mixed police forces, with careful indoctrination in handling conflict situations, can deal most effectively with open conflict, and the presence of such forces may decrease the likelihood of conflict.

92. In the event of open conflict the resolution of the crisis with a minimum of violence, damage, and residue of hostility is facilitated by:

> (a) prompt and full publicity to allay fears and to stress the control agencies' capacities to control
> (b) assurances of strict and impartial justice
> (c) special distribution of police to danger spots
> (d) provision for prompt summoning of military or other outside order-maintaining forces
> (e) enlisting cooperation of neighborhood leaders
> (f) personal public appeal by high officials
> (g) the presence of high officials in danger areas—with full dramatization of their presence
> (h) minimum use of force.

(F) *Social Organization*

93. Possibilities of conflict are lessened by the establishment of clear, detailed, and widely recognized patterns for interpersonal relationships in situations of casual contact (e.g., in public conveyances).

Example: In Detroit increasing numbers of instances of intergroup friction were noted:

> . . . in certain areas around five in the evening . . . due to the effort of workers leaving several large factories to crowd onto overloaded streetcars and busses . . . cuing up greatly reduced the amount of pushing and fighting on the loading platforms. (Watson, 210, p. 178)

94. In America a minority ethnic or racial group struggling for improved status, or for the alleviation of intergroup hostility, will be most successful if it relies upon a variety of organizations rather than one overall organization.

> In race relations, as in other problem areas, the "omnibus" type of organization has little chance to achieve real success. . . . It is entirely conceivable that a given community might well support several interracial committees, each functioning in a specific field of interest, each attracting to its membership individuals who find in the committee objective outlets for their primary interest. (Lett, 115, p. 38)

> Our conclusion will be that a suppressed minority group like the Negro people is best served by *several organizations* dividing the field and maximizing the support that can be gained from different groups of whites. (Myrdal, 154, p. 835)

95. Mediation between groups in conflict is possible only when effective appeal can be made to a superior value-consensus which transcends group differences, e.g., the preservation of a larger community, common larger "interests," basic religious values, shared mores, etc. (Suggested by L. S. Cottrell, Jr.)

96. Open conflict is rendered less likely by providing regularized leisure-time activities for those population elements most susceptible to riot-forming influences (e.g., adolescent males of lower class groups).

97. The device of *official* committees concerned with intergroup relations (e.g., Mayors' committees) will not ordinarily originate pressure for change but may be useful in transmitting pressure from more mili-

tant groups to official political leaders. (Watson, unpublished study
of intergroup action programs)

98. Outside agencies coming into a local community to stimulate,
initiate, or otherwise affect programs directed toward intergroup relations will meet minimum resistance when they: (a) work through local
persons and established local groups; (b) avoid extensive publicity for
themselves; (c) adapt techniques and organization to local circumstances
rather than propose a rigid scheme prepared in advance.

99. Aggressive needs, arising out of internal group structure, are
lessened by arrangements providing for the necessary authority and
coordination through group consensus rather than through rigid hier-
archal organization.

> Another safeguard of disruptive social phenomena is a social struc-
> ture in which the group members' cooperation is based on more
> or less free agreement with each other, and is not based on a
> coercion through a tyrannical father figure. (Alexander, 1, p. 28)

> Comparison of groups of children playing under "democratic" and
> mildly "autocratic" leadership has shown evidence of greater hos-
> tility-tension in the autocratic groups. A repressive structure can
> generate either apathy or aggression within the group. Only in
> autocratic groups were individuals used as scapegoats for focused
> aggression. (From Lewin, Lippitt and White, 122)

> [In a rigid dictatorship] . . . aggressive impulses are turned against
> the dissenting citizenry . . . the disobedient brothers and sisters . . .
> (Zilboorg, 223, p. 641)

> The more highly disciplined an army, the greater is its aggressive
> spirit against an enemy. Hence, the greater the discipline of group
> life, its repressions, privations, and exactions, either in the form of
> moral, religious, or economic sanctions, the greater may we expect
> its aggressiveness to become at the expense of some other group or
> groups. (MacCrone, 131, p. 251)

100. Dispersion of minorities as individuals or small groups (*not* as
communities) throughout a wide area and in various positions in the
social structure tends to diffuse hostility and in the long run to reduce it.

> Experience has shown that, when an individual or a few individual
> Negro families have entered high and medium income areas
> [residential], resistance to them has gradually declined. (Weaver,
> 211, p. 105)

If Jews could be evenly distributed through the social structure, anti-Semitism would probably be greatly reduced. (Parsons, 159, p. 197)

101. A vulnerable minority can itself help to reduce hostility and conflict insofar as there is group control over individual members, by:

(a) educating its members to an understanding of the dominant group's reaction to the minority's values and behavior
(b) careful study of the behaviors of its own members which are regarded as objectionable by other groups
(c) minimizing conspicuous display of traits of marked negative-symbol value
(d) participation *as individuals* in wider community activities which are widely regarded as necessary in the common welfare.

102. All other things being equal, the probability of intergroup conflict is reduced by any measures which facilitate the internal differentiation of minorities, insofar as this serves to remove the objective basis for rigid social categorization.

It is believed that these propositions constitute a reasonably solid base of reference from which future research may depart. It is believed also that they constitute a challenge of the first order to social science and social action in these times. We have a fair sampling of the problems now before us and shall next consider possible approaches to the study of these questions—approaches which must always be guided by the ultimate imperatives of developing understanding and control.

CHAPTER IV

SELECTED POSSIBILITIES FOR RESEARCH

Possible Projects [1]

So much has already been said in this report about the urgent problems which call for further intensive research that a detailed listing of possible studies is hardly necessary. In this field, as in many others, the social scientist or the practitioner is not plagued by any lack of important hypotheses; the difficulty is rather that of deciding among multiple possibilities. Yet there is some value in giving a few concrete illustrations of the types of studies which might be initiated to test certain hypotheses previously outlined. To try to specify a complete study design in each case would be not only impracticable, but would be likely to defeat its own ends as well. Worth-while research on the problems of central interest is not routine, but a flexible and inventive process. Any concrete designs outlined in advance are likely to be out of date or inappropriate in other times and circumstances. At this place accordingly, we shall simply list a limited number of diversified projects as representative of the much larger range of fruitful studies awaiting social scientists in this field. Some of these projects will then be used to illustrate feasible study designs in the second section of this chapter.

An appropriate alternative would have been to list studies which should not be made. The number of relatively trivial studies which give static descriptions of unimportant phenomena concerning restricted and atypical populations is already more than sufficient. This is especially true of some types of attitude or opinion studies.[2] Neither science nor social practice is likely to be well served, for example, by indiscriminate "polling" of school and college classes with ambiguous instruments and inadequate hypotheses. Similarly, we can well do without some of the elaborate correlational studies whose strained ex post facto interpretations have done little to increase causal understanding. Research energy needs to be more sharply focused, and there is some meaning in the

---

[1] This chapter is limited to a description of selected research opportunities, with a minimum of explicit consideration of methodological problems. Discussion of research approaches and techniques is confined to the Appendix. Readers who are mainly interested in the content of proposed types of research can thus avoid discussion of the more technical problems of research operations. Persons having a special interest in method and in specific research techniques may wish to give critical attention to materials in the Appendix.

[2] For documentation of some of the grounds for this view see Q. McNemar, "Opinion-Attitude Methodology," *Psychological Bulletin,* 43:289–374 (1946).

assertion that the quality of studies in this field is presently more important than the quantity.

There is nothing in the facts or logic of the situation to prevent excellent scientific work of great practical importance from being done within the decade. The design of good research does not differ in principle from that in any other social field; important problems abound and can be studied; there is a growing demand for usable results;[3] considerable progress in research methods and in the guiding sociological and psychological theory is evident. Given the will to undertake the necessary laborious and continuing studies and the requisite funds, advances of the first order are within reach.

The subsequent list of possible types of studies follows in the main the grouping of hypotheses in Chapter III. Many of the projects suggested are designed to throw light on the effects of specific programs of purposive action; the programs to be observed and tested, in nearly every conceivable instance, will constitute only one set of factors in a complex social situation. *It is therefore of crucial importance that research appraisals of action programs be sensitive to wider, unplanned, or "accidental" factors which may influence the behavior under observation.* A program of education on intergroup relations undertaken in a period of low social tension and good and improving economic conditions may be associated with a measurable and important decrease in intergroup hostility. There can be no a priori guarantee of the same results in a period of severe economic deprivation.[4] The effects of a program which actually increases intergroup cooperation may be completely obscured by the effects of concurrent political agitation. Examples of this kind could be listed in profusion. There is no rule for anticipating the extraneous influences which may appear in any particular situation; but one can be continually alert to such disturbing factors, and they must always be taken into account in the evaluation of specific programs.

[3] To take a random example, it is reported that at a conference of school administrators sponsored by the Bureau of Intercultural Education in March 1946, "All members said they were interested in tests or scales that would give clues to pupil attitudes and beliefs. Recognizing the limited value of paper and pencil tests, one member asked how to get at the attitudes of non-verbal groups. Believing that there were practical limitations to mass testing of pupils, another member raised the question of how to select proper samples for testing." (Bureau of Intercultural Education, *Administrators Think Together*, mimeographed, June 1946, p. 20.) Cf. this statement: "Especially important is the testing of materials and methods used in intercultural work, for in many cases the materials and methods do not result in what well-intentioned people think they do." (Everett R. Clinchy, "The Effort of Organized Religion," *The Annals*, 244:134)

[4] This reservation will hold even when control and experimental groups have been utilized: Any differential between the groups might disappear in a different socio-economic situation.

I. *General Studies: Historical, Comparative, Genetic*

1. *Comparative historical analysis of internal disturbances, either for the United States alone or on an international basis*

Much work along this line has already been done, but the possibilities for analysis of recurrent causal factors have not been exhausted. There is evidence that there are common factors in many seemingly diverse varieties of mass violence. The constant and variable factors and their interrelations may be further illuminated by a broad but intensive comparison of a series of such events as riots, lynchings, mobs, strikes with violence, insurrections, revolts, and rebellions.

This type of study requires high competence and entails a considerable measure of interdisciplinary cooperation. The contributions of historians, sociologists, psychologists, economists, and political scientists should be utilized. The main potential values of such a study appear to be three: (1) further clarification of uniformities as a basis for prediction in future situations; (2) additional perspective as to prevalence and range of variation of internal group conflicts; (3) indications as to the consequences of various "control measures" which have been put into practice in past situations.

2. *Comparative historical analysis of political anti-minority movements in the United States*

Much of the comment concerning Project 1 is applicable. Counter-movements and factors associated with the disintegration of anti-minority movements might receive special attention.

3. *Functional analysis of control and displacement of aggression in non-literate societies: a cross-cultural study*

Materials for such a study can be found in the works of anthropologists, and a systematic source of data of wide scope is available in the Cross-Cultural Survey at Yale University. The findings probably would not have a great many immediate implications for specific action. Judging from work already available, however, it is likely that we would gain further worth-while knowledge of the factors in the *total* aggression-balance of social systems, and of the range of specific control mechanisms.

4. *Patterns of prejudice interrelations within the individual personality*

To what extent and in what ways are prejudiced people prejudiced *in general* or only in relation to specific objects? Does removal of a particular scapegoat only result in fixation upon another? Are the resultants different with different basic personality structures, and why or why not? A whole series of studies are suggested by the questions which arise in connection with this topic. Methods of investigation will have to include both clinical and mass-testing approaches.

5. *Continuing study of intergroup developments accompanying large-scale action programs not ostensibly dealing with intergroup relations*

This is a general type of study rather than a specific one. Studies of this kind are certainly difficult to design and execute, but the importance of the subject warrants exploratory work in a variety of situations. It is especially important in the applications of many governmental programs to local communities. Thus, for example, the commodity-control referenda of the Agricultural Adjustment Administration resulted in large numbers of Negro farmers voting on the programs. How extensive was this voting, and how did it vary in different areas and communities? What were the factors in acceptance? What were the reactions of whites and Negroes, initially and later? Did the innovation have any transfer-quality for other situations? Another pertinent example is provided by the programs of the Tennessee Valley Authority. Directly and indirectly the TVA is having tremendous influence on the economy and social structure of a large area of the southeastern states. What connections are there, if any, between this influence and any changes in the patterns of race relations in the region? For example, how have hiring, training, and upgrading of Negro workers affected relations of white and Negro workers? Where local customs were breached, as they certainly were in some instances, what techniques were used and with what apparent results? Large-scale unionization in industry, with its emphasis on solidarity of interests among workers of various groups, provides a third illustration.

6. *Analysis of influences inculcating group prejudice in children*

Specific studies in this area can begin from several well-established generalizations, e.g., (1) prejudices are learned and therefore must be "taught"; (2) prejudices are often established at an early age (under 6 years); (3) early prejudices are *generalized* aversions with little specific content; only later are they differentiated and rationalized; (4) prejudices can be developed in the absence of direct personal contact with the disliked groups; (5) specific rewards and penalties are invoked by prejudiced elders to teach children their prejudices. There is need for detailed study of the dynamic process by which intergroup attitudes are established, using direct observation and intensive interviewing. Careful comparative study of the *specific* behaviors of relatively prejudiced vs. unprejudiced parents and teachers should be especially rewarding.

7. *Effects of a total intergroup program upon a given community*

This project would depend upon the cooperation of a local community and a national agency equipped to carry out a comprehensive local program. Probably the best locale would be a city of 25,000 to 50,000 population, containing several ethnic or racial groups, and sufficiently "typical" in industry and social structure to permit comparison with similar cities. The basic idea would be to test the over-all effects of an integrated program designed to improve intergroup relations. The specific content of the program would be worked out by the responsible parties involved, in consultation with such outside advisers and experts as seemed desirable, but presumably would include educational efforts, development of intergroup activities and organizations, changes in housing and recreational situations, efforts to change employment practices, and so on. Prior to the initiation of the program, a reasonably comparable city or cities would be selected. All the communities chosen would be surveyed at the same time to secure a comprehensive initial picture of intergroup attitudes and behaviors. After a period of, say, one year during which one community participated in the program and the others did not, a re-survey would be carried out to determine the effects of the program. It is also essential that such a study provide for intensive observation in the communities throughout the experimental period.

This is a large-scale, expensive study and it would require careful planning, a skilled staff, and close coordination of research with action and of extra-local with local groups. If properly done, however, it would give a far more dependable basis than has hitherto existed for appraising the changes which can be achieved by such a program.

8. *Comparative studies of values and behaviors of various racial, ethnic, or religious groups*

In Chapter III it was indicated that certain varieties of intergroup hostility rest *in part* upon real differences in typical systems of belief and behavior in the respective social groups. A large part of the evidence as to group similarities and differences, however, is fragmentary and impressionistic. To fill the existing gaps in knowledge would require a complex and extensive research program, but much can be added by strategic studies of the more important groups. For the purposes envisaged here these studies should not be broad general descriptions, but should be focused on specific items of difference and commonality between groups exhibiting symptoms of tension. In specific areas are there identifiable characteristics which typically, or in particular sub-groups, differentiate Negroes and whites, "old Yankees" and French-Canadian stocks, Jews and Gentiles, Catholics and Baptists, and so on? To what extent do the characteristics objectively determined by research correspond with each group's picture of itself and of the other group? To what extent and in what ways do the self-other conceptions derive from social definitions which are potentially subject to reformulation in terms less productive of hostility?

Of the important groups in the United States, the Negroes have been most adequately studied from this point of view. The least satisfactory body of evidence is that relating to religious groups.

The suggested studies would have practical significance mainly for propaganda and education programs. Research can help by (1) defining the strategic limits beyond which it is probably unwise to stress group similarities; (2) providing objective data to demonstrate internal differentiation of minorities, and to reveal discrepancies between observed characteristics and popular stereotypes; (3) identifying items of seeming difference which can be redefined as congruent; (4) inventorying important common values and behavior patterns which may not be widely known.

9. Basic survey of areas of intergroup tension

Many specific research and action projects would be facilitated by a "reconnaissance" survey to locate the specific points of intergroup contact and friction, area by area and center by center. Such a survey was proposed in 1944 in these terms:

> In order to get an over-all view of the critical points of group conflict, one research project might undertake to plot the major areas or places in the country where racial, religious, and other group differences become highly acute. This might be a continuing survey or register of data kept at one central place . . . This body of material would, in turn, provide a basis for more intensive analysis of both institutional and individual causation of prejudice in the particular areas: industry, business, education, and so on.[5]

10. Inventory of approaches and techniques in intergroup relations

With all the numerous and varied intergroup programs which have been operating for years in the United States, one still searches in vain

[5] Donald Young and Kimball Young, *Notes on Research in the Field of Group Prejudice* (mimeographed, December 1944), p. 1.

for a systematic account of specific action approaches. Published accounts are in such general terms that only persons already familiar with the situations described can visualize exactly what was done. There is immediate need for a systematic, concrete, and detailed inventory of the actual events usually connoted by such terms as "educating," "organizing," "persuading," and the like.

This reconnaissance project could be undertaken on a national scale over a period of years. A suitable sponsor might well be a national action agency with a legitimate concern in promoting the interchange of valuable experiences among organizations working on intergroup problems. The type of information necessary could not be adequately obtained by widely circulated questionnaires or other extensive survey methods. It would probably require persistent and intensive interviewing by experts and detailed observation in the field.

Beyond such relatively specific studies as those just suggested, there is a clear need for fundamental re-examination, on a high level, of the role of persistent structural factors in group hostility. What are the basic interconnections between intergroup hostility or conflict and the legal structure, the system of property relations and economic exchange, and the dominant constellations of political power? To take only one illustration, is it yet clear to what extent and in what ways modern racism is dependent on a specific historical situation of colonial expansion and associated economic practices? There have been sweeping and dogmatic answers, as well as scholarly and comprehensive studies, but it is very doubtful whether the possibilities for fundamental analysis have been fully explored. Fruitful work at this level is most likely to be the product of exceptional factual knowledge and theoretical insight on the part of rare individuals. Hence a listing of projects seems inappropriate. However, it would be inexcusable to overlook the need for such broad analysis since it alone can provide the context for deriving maximum significance from the more detailed empirical research now to be outlined.

II. *Effects of Information, Education, and Propaganda* [6]

11. *Audiences reached and their reactions to mass educational and propagandist materials*

Little is known as to the audiences actually reached by materials designed to affect intergroup relations. Unpublished studies and informal

[6] The writer is indebted to Dr. Everett R. Clinchy of the National Conference of Christians and Jews for a number of suggestions regarding this area of study.

observation suggest that many materials reach a restricted audience, consisting mainly of "people of good will," and that many items disseminated on a mass basis are often poorly understood or misunderstood.

The specific materials awaiting analysis are legion: (a) books, articles, news items, pamphlets, cartoons, comics; (b) plays, skits, pageants, etc.; (c) motion pictures; (d) radio programs; (e) speeches, forums, panels, etc. Up to the present time judgments on the effectiveness of given types of materials have been almost entirely in the realm of opinion.

Studies of three types are possible: (1) Content analysis of the materials can reveal pervading themes and emphases, which can then be evaluated on the basis of accepted knowledge and assumptions, or in relation to the findings of the other two types of analysis. (2) For description of the size and nature of audiences reached, adequate data on readers and listeners can only be obtained by careful use of specialized techniques. Personal interviews, using tests of recall, will usually be necessary to determine which individuals have seen, read, or listened to given items. (3) For analysis of effects upon an audience, a sample survey *after* it has been reached can elicit some indications of the degrees of liking and disliking, the reasons for each, and retrospective accounts of change or lack of change in attitudes and behavior. If the sample of readers or listeners could be carefully matched with a sample of nonreaders or nonlisteners, an after-test of attitudes for which the groups showed significant differences might demonstrate that the materials did affect the attitudes of those reached. A still more rigorous procedure would involve before-and-after testing of experimental and control groups.

Because of the large audiences involved and because of the great emphasis upon mass education and propaganda in action programs, this area of research is of prime practical importance. The testing of reactions to motion pictures and nationally circulated articles, advertisements, etc. warrants an especially high priority.

12. *Relative effectiveness of alternative media for mass education and propaganda*

A series of comparative studies is required in order to do justice to this field. With a given body of information and set of appeals to be presented, what differences in mass effects can be expected from the use of radio vs. motion pictures, pamphlets vs. magazine articles, and so on? There are some general research findings and a large body of experience, of varying dependability, in the market research field which can be drawn upon in designing studies to answer such questions. The difficulties are considerable but not insurmountable. Adequate results depend upon knowing the audience reached, and the effects upon it. This will usually require a combination of the mass sample survey with careful experimental studies of small groups.

13. *Differential effects of alternative types of propaganda appeals*

Probably the most important practical problem in this area concerns the effects of "ethical" appeals emphasizing morality, fair play, duty, or conscience, compared with the effects of "conciliatory" appeals emphasizing shared values, mutual interests, and the like. There is absolutely no experimental evidence on this problem. It probably should be approached by giving carefully chosen materials to groups matched on initial attitudes or other behavioral indexes, e.g., a control group, a group receiving one type of material, a group receiving alternative material, and a fourth sample being exposed to both. After-tests would then be used to determine any shifts in over-all attitudes and behavior. In addition, it would be important to carry out intensive interviews. Studies of this kind should not be restricted to analysis of a single presentation. The more significant problem is that of the effects of a *program* of one type or another carried out over a period of time.

14. *Comparison of behavioral and opinion changes associated with contrasting types of teaching on intergroup relations*

The basic purpose would be to test the differential effectiveness of complex *types* of instruction, rather than of single techniques. A useful experiment could be devised along these lines: Establish one teaching program which takes a "factual" approach, relies exclusively upon textbooks and other written materials as sources, is restricted to the classroom, and uses mainly the lecture method. Establish a contrasting program including the following "progressive" methods: (1) encouragement of group discussion and catharsis, (2) presentation of facts in terms of emotional and value implications, (3) use of motion pictures and other visual aids, (4) field experience in intergroup matters. The variables of class composition and personality of instructors would have to be controlled. For instance, the most rigorous design might involve comparisons of the results of the two methods as applied by instructors with contrasting personalities and intergroup attitudes, and of results when the same instructor uses the two programs with comparable groups.

15. *Effects of role-taking upon attitudes and behavior*

Both ordinary drama and "psychodrama" techniques are sometimes thought to affect persons playing certain roles in them. Does participation in a psychodrama enactment of intergroup situations involve sufficient emotional reaction and restructuring to show appreciable effects? We do not know, but it would not be too difficult to find out. A conventional before-and-after design is indicated, with retests to check the persistence of effects should measurable changes be found.

16. *Effectiveness of a program of education in intergroup relations for public officials*

Training of police forces, for example, has been carried on in San Francisco, Boston, Passaic, Louisville, Cincinnati, Washington, and other cities. The kinds of observation and measurement which may be feasible will vary with local circumstances, but worth-while evidence can undoubtedly be collected in some instances.

17. *Effects of "workshop" training in intergroup relations upon teachers' opinions and performance*

Intensive brief training programs of the workshop type enjoy wide popularity, and potential opportunities for testing their effects are correspondingly numerous. From a practical standpoint, comparative study of the effects of different *kinds* of workshop training is likely to be most rewarding.

18. *Effects of specific training programs upon intergroup behavior of community leaders*

A comprehensive study in this area is currently being carried out by the Research Center for Group Dynamics of the Massachusetts Institute of Technology, in cooperation with a state interracial commission. The results of this research will undoubtedly furnish valuable evidence as to the specific study design likely to be most practicable.

19. *Effects of adult education programs of religious organizations*

The work of the National Conference of Christians and Jews with women's groups is a ready illustration of a widespread type of activity which deserves research testing.

20. *Effects of religious teachings upon attitudes of children toward other groups*

Here is another unexplored area of study. In Sunday Schools the teaching materials of many denominations recently have begun to emphasize intergroup relations. It would be possible to secure at least some indications of effects by comparing groups using such materials with properly matched groups not using them, and comparing both in turn with children not receiving Sunday School training. Significant variables to be controlled would include geographic region, size of community, socio-economic class, and ethnic stock, as well as age and sex. To isolate in part the factor of family influence, which may overlap with "religious training," it might be possible to compare childrens' attitudes with those of their parents in each type of group studied.

A related project would be the testing of attitudes accompanying training in parochial schools. Since the total social milieu of Catholic families is likely to differ in some ways from that of other groups, the most defensible procedure would probably be to combine several tangential lines of evidence. One approach would be to compare attitudes of different age-groups passing through the parochial system. Simultaneously, any Catholic children attending public schools should be tested— with proper control groups. Third, comparisons with roughly equated groups of children receiving (and not receiving) other kinds of religious training would be in order. To be most useful such studies should not stop with measurement of differentials, but should analyze the factors likely to be responsible for observed differences.

21. *Effects of joint Christian-Jewish religious education upon Jewish-Gentile relations*

Joint services and educational programs have been undertaken in a number of instances. Through established organizations it should be possible to arrange for before-and-after tests of participants, and for other observations of community reactions.

22. *Majority group reactions to changes in minority behavior*

Careful research should be able to throw some light on this area of heated controversy. Are stereotypes changed by actual changes in the behavior of minority representatives? Many people seem to think so, when they suggest programs of self-education and self-discipline for minorities. Others cite such cases as the persecution of thoroughly "assimilated" Jews in Germany as evidence that stereotypes are not dependent upon objective behavior.

One possible project would involve finding a situation in which a local program of minority self-education in "acceptable" behaviors was to be initiated, e.g., in a department store, factory, school system, or whole community. Before-and-after measurements of minority attitudes and behavior should be secured and a program of intensive observation of majority group reactions should be carried out. Such a project would extend over a considerable period of time, since any appreciable changes would not be expected immediately. Great care and ingenuity would be required in order to insure objective observations. Also, tact and skill would be essential in dealing with the many complicated problems of intergroup and interpersonal relations necessarily involved.

23. *Differential reactions to materials for education and propaganda among various classes and sectional groups*

Can it be assumed that a uniform program of mass communication is generally applicable, or should different materials and themes be directed at various sectors of the population? The best a priori guess would seem to be the latter. If so, what are the significant groups and what types of programs are likely to be most effective with each? The only type of study adequate for answering such questions at the national level involves, first of all, careful nation-wide sampling to secure reliable data on all major groups. It should certainly be stratified by educational and economic levels, and should adequately represent Southern, Southwestern, Far Western, and Northeastern areas having distinctive minority problems. It may be desirable to select a number of representative samples for simultaneous study. Each sample would be tested for responses to a given type of appeal, e.g., emotional vs. factual, ethical vs. self-interest, with materials of graded levels of complexity applied to whatever minority was of special interest.

24. *Effects of intergroup education in summer camps sponsored by religious organizations*

Although this is a relatively minor activity in the total field of intergroup education, it furnishes another specific and feasible opportunity for research and the findings of studies would be of considerable practical interest to agencies working with children and young people. There are certainly over a hundred such camps in the United States. In many of them intergroup education is received by only part of the camp population and the selection of individuals is essentially random. Thus, experimental and control groups are in part ready for testing.

25. *An experiment on group influence upon individuals' attitudes in an educational situation*

Several variations can be set up. In one study design the experimental factor will be knowledge of the attitudes of others in the group. Thus, one of two matched classes equated on initial attitudes might be informed of its own group opinion while the other class would not be. Identical programs of instruction and experience would be followed in the two groups, and the outcomes tested. Or, the two groups might be given opposite evaluations of the group opinion, e.g., "high and increasing prejudice" versus "little and decreasing prejudice."

Another type of study would investigate the influence of group decision, the major hypothesis being that it results in greater and more stable changes than individual decisions. An experimental group would be required to reach a decision regarding specific policy in improving intergroup relations in a local area. A control group would be treated exactly the same except that individuals would give separate and anonymous decisions.

26. Analysis of content of and reactions to school textbooks

The most useful results would be obtained by combining content analysis of the materials with intensive study of responses of students. To what extent do textbooks in common use contain materials prejudicial to various ethnic, racial, and religious groups? [7] What specific reactions are elicited in pupils, and what are the prevalence and intensity of each type of response? The latter question is open to at least two main approaches. One would compare the attitudes of students who have and who have not been exposed to a given body of materials—with the best possible equating of background factors and instructional situations. The second approach would utilize intensive focused interviews to explore the qualitative dimensions of reactions, to identify salient materials, and to reveal the detailed processes by which given materials elicit various individual responses.

27. Observational study of intergroup practices in particular schools and school systems

This is in one sense an exploratory study rather than one designed to test a sharply defined hypothesis. Precise observations of daily interaction of groups in school situations have not yet been published, if they have been made. Such observations for a series of situations, ranging from intense intolerance to relative absence of prejudice, would probably be of great value in revealing possibly significant differential factors and clarifying our understanding of the actual processes by which intergroup cooperation and tolerance are built up or intergroup hostility and conflict encouraged.

---

[7] Some studies have already been made. Content analysis along these lines has also been applied to radio programs and motion pictures.

III. *Effects of Personal Contacts*

28. *Effects of types and degrees of segregation on intergroup attitudes*

Establishment of the effects of segregation per se will be an extraordinarily difficult task. Valid conclusions of high generality will probably have to await the accumulation of many studies of varying local situations, but any systematic evidence which can be discovered will constitute an improvement over the present state of knowledge of this fundamentally significant subject.

One feasible project, worthy of extensive repetition, is a comparative study of intergroup relations in segregated and mixed areas of the same community. Even in Southern cities there are "fringe" areas which could be systematically observed. Where is friction greatest? Where are the areas of high and low intensity and incidence of verbal prejudice? How do stable areas of intermingling compare with shifting areas and with "invasion" points? It will be necessary, of course, to match the samples studied as closely as possible, especially with respect to socioeconomic status; usually only rough approximations can be expected.

29. *Effects of participation in a mixed Negro-white Boy or Girl Scout troop*

For controlled comparison of changes in attitude, each mixed group would be matched with, say, two white control groups. Before-and-after tests should be given to both experimental and control groups, with follow-up tests after a period of time.

30. *Changes in attitudes and behavior accompanying experiences in interracial or other intergroup camps*

Various camps sponsored by civic agencies, religious groups, and other private organizations include members of different racial, religious, and ethnic groups. The fact that camp experiences are defined as recreation might be expected to induce a "free" psychological set conducive to lability in behavior. Before-and-after testing plus direct observation may often be relatively simple; follow-up tests and other observation should be carried out whenever possible, in order to secure evidence on persistence of changes.

31. *Changes in attitudes and behavior accompanying participation in an interracial housing project*

One study design in this area is outlined in the Appendix (pp. 110–111) as an illustration of methods. The ideal design would entail before-and-after measurements of experimental and control groups, but ex post facto testing can approximate such a projected experiment. Lacking these two possibilities, suggestive evidence may be secured from comparative study of characteristics of applicants, turnover rates, reports of participant observers on sequences of change, surveys using brief interviews or questionnaires, and intensive interviewing of representative samples.

32. *An experiment in social contact as a means of modifying attitudes of white college or high-school students toward Negroes*

F. Tredwell Smith's study [8] is often cited as the classic example of a good design in this particular field. Yet his sample was a highly selected one and the experiment was carried out under circumstances rather different from those found in other areas. There remains a definite need for further studies of more nearly "typical" groups under other local conditions. In the ordinary course of events a great many students each year are taken on field trips, visit Negro families and other groups, and participate in bi-racial activities. Since student populations are easily accessible for the researcher, no deliberate rearrangements of group practice are necessary for such studies.

33. *Comparative studies of industrial or other plants employing mixed labor forces*

At least three main approaches are possible. The first requires finding an instance in which members of a minority are to be introduced into plants, departments, or jobs in which they have not previously been employed. An initial "survey"—not necessarily on a formalized mass basis—would be made to secure a base for measurements taken at a later period; care would be necessary to insure that the attempt at observation did not itself become a factor in employee reactions. The second approach would compare similar work situations, some employing mixed groups, others not. The fruitfulness of such comparisons would depend upon the closeness with which the contrasting situations could be equated as to such factors as type of jobs, income, stability of employment, composition of the labor force, personnel policies, and union-management relations. The third possibility is that of comparing relatively "successful" and "unsuccessful" instances in which minority group members have been employed in new work areas.[9]

---

[8] *An Experiment in Modifying Attitudes toward the Negro* (New York: Teachers College, Columbia University, 1943).

[9] For a rough sketch of a possible study design see pp. 97–99.

Opportunities for studies of this type depend to an important degree upon the potential usefulness of their results in solving practical problems, and upon the confidence which can be established that the research will be done with social skill and tact.

The employment of Negroes in plants which had hitherto used only white labor was an extensive wartime development. Many bi-racial work forces exist, permitting at least *current* comparisons. The possibility of before-and-after studies, of course, is contingent upon the extent to which integrated work forces are created in the future.

34. *Effects of sociometric rearrangement of mixed school populations*

Some teachers have suggested that the clusters of interpersonal associations and preferences in schools containing minority and majority members can be manipulated to minimize group cleavage and prejudice. For example, seating arrangements in classrooms, study halls, and cafeterias could put minority "isolates" into association with the "stars" in other groups, cut across clique lines based on ethnic membership, and so on. Such procedures have been put into practice in at least a few cases. The possibilities for observation and testing are good. Although large changes are hardly to be anticipated from such limited group rearrangements, specific studies would be relatively simple and inexpensive and would add to knowledge of the mechanisms and limits of control of intergroup relations.

35. *Analysis of interracial churches*

Several prominent interracial churches recently have been established in urban centers. What are the characteristics of the participants? What are the reactions upon the larger community? Do the participants show any changes in behavior and attitudes? Questions of this order merit study as occasion permits.

36. *Reactions of white patients to interracial contacts in hospitals*

This problem includes reactions of patients to both hospital staffs and experiences in mixed wards. A few large urban hospitals provide both types of experience. Probably the most feasible kind of study would consist of interviews with former patients to explore their reactions on an intensive level.

IV. *Effects of Legal Enactments, Law-Enforcement Activities, and Political "Pressure" Tactics*

37. *Reactions to anti-discrimination legislation or judicial decisions*

The specific kinds of stimuli to be studied range from national FEPC or Supreme Court rulings to local municipal ordinances. The data to be sought consist of objective records of behavior on the one hand, and expressed opinions on the other. On both counts "informed opinions" will be a useful supplementary source of understanding. Depending upon the particular investigation, objective data should be obtained on such items as: (1) intergroup incidents and use of violence (from community observers, court records); (2) discriminatory advertisements, e.g., employment or real estate; (3) extent and types of employment of minority members; (4) minority members holding public offices; (5) extent of voting by minority members in political elections; (6) their participation in various "social" organizations; (7) patronage of minority members at commercial establishments formerly restricted to a majority clientele. To illustrate only one of these items: the Ives-Quinn legislation in New York State forbids certain discriminatory practices in employment. It may be possible in some instances to analyze pay roll records before and after the passage of this legislation, and thus to determine any changes in the ethnic and racial distribution of persons engaged in various industries and occupations. An alternative procedure would be to secure work histories from samples of various groups in the community at large. The preferable source of data concerning opinions would be a survey of a representative sample of the population, perhaps with expanded subsamples of such groups as employers, supervisors, union leaders, public officials. *Awareness* of the legal provisions should be tested, as well as specific evaluative opinions. Supplementary sources include editorials and other journalistic reactions, and resolutions and other expressions of opinion by organized groups. Minority as well as majority population elements should be sampled.

The ideal situation for research of this kind is one permitting direct comparisons of tests and retests. When it can be foreseen that anti-discrimination rulings or enactments are likely to appear in a given area, research plans should be ready to take advantage of the event. Failing this (perhaps utopian) condition, much valuable evidence can still be obtained from systematic observation after the fact.

38. *Analysis of reactions of local labor unions to nondiscriminatory regulations of national unions*

In unions connected with the Congress for Industrial Organization and in certain others, the pressure for nondiscriminatory practices tends to flow "from the top down." Various specific methods are used to bring pressure on local unions. Evaluation of the reactions is greatly to be desired. Perhaps the most practicable source of data for analysis would be a series of case studies in which the process was followed over a period of time. Unionization in the South, as in the Birmingham area, offers a particularly valuable situation for study.

39. *Analysis of reactions to mass demonstrations for minority rights*

What actually are the reactions of various elements of the population to such events as the rally against G. L. K. Smith in Los Angeles and the projected "March on Washington" of Negro organizations advocating fair employment regulations? Certain factual accompaniments, such as the actual securing of the definite objectives of a demonstration, can be judged to be effects. In addition, systematic evidence as to less direct effects upon attitudes and behavior would be very valuable. Intensive interviewing would be a required part of research on this problem.

40. *Analysis of voting of legislators on intergroup issues*

In a period of unprecedented agitation for various legal changes bearing on intergroup relations, there is a rich field for study of the political realities involved in the control of intergroup discrimination and conflict. A first crude approximation to understanding might be secured through correlating legislative voting on specific issues (FEPC, poll tax, anti-discrimination, anti-lynching, school appropriations, etc.) with the known characteristics of the effective constituency of individual legislators. These characteristics would include the proportions of various ethnic, racial, and religious groups, and of urban and rural residents, traditional party affiliations and extent of split-ticket voting, economic class, etc. A second approximation might come from a careful examination of the specific pressure groups operating in each situation. Legislative hearings frequently provide initial clues in this area, and these can be followed up by more detailed study of the participants. A third step would be to analyze the actual process whereby various "pressures" were translated into legislative action.

This project obviously should be carried out by persons having intimate knowledge of, and access to, particular legislative bodies. Its potential values are (1) in communicating a more exact knowledge of the possibilities, limitations, and effective methods of legislation for action purposes; (2) in increasing our understanding of the causal factors underlying intergroup relations in specific areas.

V. Social Organization and Programs for Reducing General Tension

41. Effectiveness of alternative programs for integrating minority group members into a work situation

Studies in this area have been suggested by Proposition 87 in Chapter III. Since it is unlikely that responsible officials will vary their methods to meet the conditions of a projected experiment, research must rely upon discovering methods which have been or will be utilized in the ordinary course of events. It may be possible to find reasonably comparable situations in which contrasting techniques of organization and control are used. Systematic comparisons of the results would be of great significance for one of the major problem areas of intergroup relations.

42. Effectiveness of alternative programs for integrating minority members into a residential area

Studies of public housing projects would be most likely to yield clear-cut findings. However, there are many unplanned situations which conceivably could be used for research, e.g., comparison of urban areas of minority "invasion" where there is an action program designed to minimize tension with similar areas in which there is no such program.

43. Attitudes and behavior of two types of interracial committees

Both types of committees would have mixed membership and would be matched in as many other relevant respects as possible, but one type would be explicitly interracial and the emphasis of its work would be upon interracial relations. The work of the other type would be directed toward community problems such as housing, recreation, health, and employment, with minimal reference to interracial aspects. Probably at least six carefully selected committees would have to be observed to allow for unavoidable imperfections in control.

To ascertain changes in attitudes over a period, committee members would be interviewed at intervals of perhaps three months. A community observer would collect all possible information on the activities of the committee and on community reactions.

Selected Illustrations of Study Design

The brief annotations of the preceding list of possible topics for re-search suggest only the broadest outlines of study design. Although it is not desirable here to specify detailed study plans, development of a few illustrative projects in somewhat more detail may be helpful. It should be emphasized, however, that these illustrations do not in any sense constitute "models" for specific studies.

A. *Study of Contributing Factors in Successful and Unsuccessful Attempts To Integrate Negroes into Industrial Plants*

(1) Secure preliminary descriptions of a series of cases in which an attempt was made (a) to introduce Negro workers into plants not having previously or recently employed them, or (b) to bring them into depart-ments or jobs in which they had not previously or recently worked, or (c) to increase greatly the number of Negroes or their proportion of the labor force in plants, departments, or jobs.

(2) Ascertain by field study the "successful" and "unsuccessful" in-stances. As criteria use: number of incidents of personal friction; com-plaints of whites and Negroes about the other group to management or union officials; upgrading of Negroes; acceptance of Negro super-visors by whites; segregated or common activities and facilities; labor turnover and absenteeism, especially in the period of transition to a mixed labor force; participation in mixed groups off-the-job (athletic teams, informal association, etc.); production records; and other similar relevant items on which information can be obtained.

(3) On the basis of the data thus collected, select as large a number as feasible of highly successful and markedly less successful cases.

(4) For each plant included in the two groups describe the major, theoretically relevant circumstances surrounding the employment of Negroes. The aim will be to match cases, insofar as possible, on those hypothetically significant factors which were not subjected to manipula-tion by management or unions for the purpose of affecting intergroup relations. Variables to be controlled could include such items as: charac-teristics of the white labor force (e.g., regional or ethnic origin, levels of education and skill, age and sex composition); presence or absence of labor union, type of union, recency of organization; wage levels and wage differentials among various jobs; housing and transportation con-ditions; stability of employment levels; community structure and history as related to group interaction.

(5) With plants reasonably well matched on these variables, detailed study of the differences in manipulated factors as between successful and unsuccessful cases may yield fairly clear causal inferences. Examples of the types of inquiries necessary to specify the nature and values of the manipulable variables include:

(a) What were the initial and later characteristics of the Negro labor force (e.g., geographic region of origin, level of education, previous industrial experience and skills, age and sex composition)?

(b) By whom was the introduction or integration of Negro workers initially proposed and under what circumstances (e.g., by union, management, or government officials; as persuasion or as edict; as a reaction to acute labor scarcity)?

(c) At what rate were Negroes brought in and in what concentrations (e.g., en masse or in small numbers at first, increasing later; concentrated in certain departments or scattered; concentrated in the more menial jobs or otherwise)?

(d) How and by whom and under what circumstances was the proposal presented to the white workers? Was it presented to a large group or to small ones or to individuals? By high or low management officials, or by high or low union officials, or by both? As a "disagreeable necessity," "a necessity but also desirable," etc. (Was the official stand firm? How much "ideological" emphasis was given?)

(e) How and by whom and under what circumstances were Negroes recruited and oriented to the work situation?

(f) What was the role of governmental regulations and governmental assistance or pressure?

(g) What were the policies and practices with regard to upgrading and to supervisory roles of minority group members?

(h) What were the policies and practices with regard to segregation?

(i) What practices were employed to deal with any instances of intergroup aggression or friction?

(j) What attempts, if any, were made to change tension-producing factors in the community (e.g., in housing, transportation, recreation, hostile publicity or agitation)?

(k) What attempts, if any, were made to direct (encourage, discourage, modify) the nature and extent of off-the-job interaction between members of the respective groups?

(l) What efforts, if any, were made in the nature of a continuing program of intergroup education or indoctrination? What were the specific media and content of any such efforts?

(m) What events outside the immediate community seem to have affected the local intergroup situation?

(n) What other specific variables appear relevant, on the basis of reconnaissance study?

(6) The large number of conceivably important factors which can thus be listed on the basis of common-sense knowledge indicates that objective appraisal of the weight of various specific action-techniques will be complex and difficult. Such appraisal, however, will certainly gain from the systematic comparison suggested. The possibilities of definitive conclusions will vary of course with the degree to which situations can be compared when only one or a few factors differ. Should it not be possible to locate reasonably well-matched cases, the same type of comparative study could still be carried out. The certainty of conclusions would be less, but there should still be important findings with a useful degree of validity.

B. *Effects of an "Ideal" Program of Education in Intergroup Relations*

This project can be carried out in any situation where it is possible to establish the educational setting outlined below. It is suggested by the recent convergence of expert opinion regarding a set of interrelated principles for any re-education which involves changing established behavior patterns and crystallized emotional tendencies. According to this opinion the most effective educational process for the reduction of intergroup prejudices will include such principles as the following:

1. It will provide for initial guided catharsis of hostile attitudes in a permissive but calm and objective setting.

2. It will work with a face-to-face group which learns as a group and not as an aggregate of isolated individuals.

3. Provision will be made for *active* learning through group participation, especially in specific role-taking experiences in "real" or "as if" situations.

4. Insofar as possible the facts to be imparted will be ascertained through the learners' own efforts.

5. Maximum closeness to real situations will be provided through visual aids, field trips, personal contacts, and direct observation.

6. There will be opportunities for discussion and concrete group decisions as to ideas, attitudes, and behavior.

The basic procedure in a study of such an "ideal" program, whether it is carried out in a single course or other educational experience, is direct observation of attitudes and behavior of an experimental group and control groups before and after exposure of the former to the program. The experimental and control groups must be matched on at least the following factors: age, sex, racial or national stock, religion, socio-economic class, and intelligence or scholastic attainment. In addition, it would be desirable to have the groups roughly equated in initial prejudices. The most comprehensive experimental design would include these types of groups: (a) experimental (given the ideal program); (b) a group given an ordinary lecture and reading course; (c) a group receiving no formal instruction. In the first two, instruction should be given by the same person or persons or else a sufficient number of groups should be used to randomize the possible influence of different personalities and approaches. To be of maximum value the study should provide for follow-up testing at two or more intervals after the experiment.

The specific hypotheses of the study are:

1. The two educational programs will result in measurable changes in attitude and behavior, as shown by comparison of instructed and uninstructed groups.

2. The ideal program will produce greater changes than the ordinary lecture and reading program.

3. The effects of the ideal program will be more persistent than those of the ordinary one.

The significance of any observed differences would be tested, of course, by appropriate statistical techniques. In addition, a continuing detailed record of the total social context of the experiment should be kept.

Extensive repetition of this study under varying circumstances is warranted because it deals with concrete situations, full of subtle and imperfectly controlled variables. Repetitive observation might well lead to the discovery and control of important factors hitherto unrecognized.

C. *Effects of Recreational Opportunities upon Intergroup Hostility among Urban Adolescent Males*

This project could be set up to deal with any or all of the intergroup conflicts affecting major ethnic, racial, and religious groups. On the most comprehensive scale it might include studies in the following areas:

> A fringe area of mixed Negro and white neighborhoods in Harlem
> A comparable area in Detroit, Chicago, or Atlanta
> An area of Jewish-Gentile conflict in New York, Baltimore, or Minneapolis
> An area of Protestant-Catholic conflict, probably drawn along ethnic lines

An area of conflict between Mexican or other Spanish American groups and "native" elements (Los Angeles would probably be the best testing ground).

The experimental program might be one of several types, depending upon available organizations, resources, and other circumstances. It might be concerned with organized recreation alone, or with recreational activities which were part of a comprehensive community effort directed toward the improvement of various aspects of intergroup relations. Also, the community program might be stimulated or carried out by an organization from outside the local area, or it might be a local effort, or both. For purposes of experimental control a program under the general direction of a national organization would be desirable. The type of program will not affect the basic study design, which is as follows:

(1) In each city studied select census tract areas or wards as nearly comparable as possible with respect to demographic characteristics, proportions of ethnic, racial, and religious groups, economic level, extent and types of formal social organization, recreational facilities, and general social type (working-class zone, transition business area, etc.). The closeness of matching of areas will be crucial and must be done with great care after intensive, detailed study.

(2) Given closely comparable areas, measure the prevalence of intergroup hostility and conflict among adolescent boys. It will be desirable to have at least three experimental and three control areas in each situation studied. Measurements should be taken on a random sample of all males between the ages of 12 and 18 to 21. The samples must be large enough to provide groups of adequate size when sorted by age, education, and other possibly significant variables. Three testing procedures should be employed: (a) Intensive interviewing should be directed toward revealing hypotheses and securing evidence for interpretation of questionnaire responses. (b) Questionnaires, using attitude scales, should be used to index prejudice toward groups in the community. If possible, questionnaires should be identified in code to preserve anonymity and yet permit later comparisons of attitudes of individuals. (c) Intergroup behavior should be observed by at least two persons trained to record all instances of group conflict and cooperation, including detailed descriptions of behavior and full reports of conversations. The observers will remain in the community during the full course of the study, making a continuing record of their observations.

(3) For the three control groups there will be no directed change in the recreational situation.

(4) For the three experimental groups a systematic program of organized recreation will be inaugurated. The specific content, of course, will depend in part upon local exigencies. Two basic types of programs are conceivable: (a) Facilities (e.g., club rooms, bowling alleys, summer camps, baseball diamond, swimming pool) and organizational help could be provided for the "dominant" group alone, or for both groups separately. Any diminution of group hostility or conflict which might accompany such a program would be attributable to a decrease in the general tension level, or to diversion of activity into harmless channels, or to a decrease in intergroup contacts, or to some combination of these. (b) A program involving some degree of association between the two groups could be initiated. This might range from athletic contests to sharing of supervised facilities or to fully integrated participation.

(5) Regardless of the type of program, the systematic records of resident observers will be used to trace developments. (The program might well include a recreational director, especially skilled in group work, working closely with one or more research assistants.) At the end of six to twelve months, a complete after-test by questionnaire and interview will be administered to the original sample, in all control and experimental groups. At least one further test will be made at the end of one to two years.

The following results may be anticipated:

(a) Measureable changes will be small. It is therefore essential that the utmost care be used in sampling, design of tests, and recording of all information which might aid in the interpretation of results.

(b) Insofar as changes are detected, they will be in the direction of lessened conflict, and probably less frequent expression of prejudice and hostility.

(c) Detailed observations and interviews will provide clues as to specific factors in change or lack of change—clues which will open up possibilities for more nearly adequate analysis. Insofar as this occurs, the study might develop into a continuing action-research program.

D. *A Comparative Study of Unionized and Non-Unionized Plants of the Same Specific Industrial Type*

So far as can be ascertained from literature available at this writing, there has been no systematic objective study of the effects of specific types of unionization upon the intergroup relations of union members and of the larger community. In American unionism a rather sharp cleavage in orientation toward intergroup relations is apparent between certain discriminatory craft-type unions, composed of skilled "aristocrats of labor" and maintaining close control over entrance into a given trade, and some of the industrial unions with explicit nondiscrimination policies.[10]

A study design illustrative of research possibilities starts from the central hypothesis that industrial unionism, emphasizing nondiscrimination and solidarity of workers, does or does not appreciably reduce hostility among workers of different racial, religious, or ethnic groups. A series of related specific hypotheses would undoubtedly emerge from the initiation of a test of this central hypothesis. (Possible effects upon worker-employer relations should certainly be considered.) It must be stressed that "unionization" is a label for an exceedingly varied set of activities and relationships. It covers educational and persuasive activities, as well as alterations in economic interests and power relations. Research in this field therefore must specify in detail just what unionization means in the situation under study.

In this study design two basic approaches are practicable. The static approach involves a cross-sectional comparison of plants at a given time. It might be feasible to compare a number of unionized and non-unionized plants in a given industry, each plant being paired with another reasonably comparable in size and location, rates of pay, composition of working force (e.g., age, sex, education, group origin), and similar relevant factors. The specific unions involved in each unionized plant would have to be characterized in detail. The paired plants might well include the following five types: no union, adaptation of employee-representation plan or company union, independent union, craft union, industrial union. Given a number of plants of two or more of these types, the procedure would be to obtain systematic evidence on and make a comprehensive analysis of intergroup relations, including behavior on the job, behavior outside the plant in the total community situation, and attitudes. Although more difficult to carry out, the dynamic approach would have the advantage of clarifying specific processes whereby intergroup relations are changed or maintained. This approach necessitates finding and gaining access to several plants in an area or industry undergoing unionization, and then following developments over a period. At least three systematic inventories of attitudes should be made: one before unionization is attempted, a second shortly after

[10] See Herbert R. Northrup, "Unions and Negro Employment," *The Annals*, 244:42–47 (1946); and *Organized Labor and the Negro* (New York: Harper & Brothers, 1944).

unions have been established, and a third at the end of one to three years of union experience. Along with these periodic measurements should go continuing intensive observation of changes in unionized plants. Concurrently, it would be valuable to study any comparable firms, plants, or industries in which unions had not developed. Thus, if it were found that intergroup hostility decreased after unionization, whereas prejudice increased or remained constant in comparable non-unionized plants (if such existed), the inference that the former effect was attributable to change in organization of workers would be justified.

CHAPTER V

SUMMARY AND PROSPECT

What findings have emerged from this survey of the current situation of research on intergroup relations and the prospects for future research? The salient points may be summarized as follows:

(1) Intergroup tensions in the United States are persistent, widespread, and serious. (Chapter I)

(2) There is much organized activity intended to reduce hostility, to promote intergroup association and cooperation, or to minimize or eliminate conflict. Interest in and concern with intergroup relations are widespread and intense. (Chapter I)

(3) The working assumptions of action programs are subject to definition and specification, but these assumptions generally have not been validated by research. In particular, the possibilities and limits of given methods of control have not been scientifically delimited; and the comparative effectiveness of various actual and potential approaches to the control of intergroup relations is unknown. (Chapter II)

(4) Existing studies show that certain types of communication and contact are effective in changing intergroup attitudes. The available findings, however, are not adequate to answer many of the more important practical questions; and they likewise leave crucial theoretical problems unanswered. (Chapter II)

(5) These findings indicate that there are urgent needs for further systematic research.

(6) Hypotheses warranting research testing have been formulated as suggestive leads for study. These hypotheses point to the definite possibility of an integrated theory for the explanation of relations among ethnic, racial, and religious groups. (Chapter III)

(7) A number of feasible research approaches and techniques have been developed in this field and are currently undergoing intensive examination and revision. Many serious inadequacies are apparent, but potential improvements are already evident. (See the Appendix.)

(8) A wide range of significant topics appear ready for fruitful research. (Chapter IV)

(9) Among practitioners in the field of intergroup relations there is a growing interest in research which is relevant to action needs. (Chapters I and IV)

These statements and their supporting materials perhaps constitute a sufficient body of research suggestions. The next step is the crucial one: the translation of suggested hypotheses and projects into careful, repeated, thoughtful research. Only from the results of future studies can we judge the validity of the appraisals made in the present monograph.

One final word may be added concerning the results which can reasonably be expected from the types of research herein suggested. Research is not magic. It can not be expected invariably to produce solutions to immediate problems, nor to formulate panaceas for social ills. Good research usually results in tentative, limited, and qualified findings—a characteristic not always appreciated by persons grappling with practical problems and strongly convinced of their seriousness and urgency. Yet it is an unavoidable characteristic, if we are to develop valid knowledge. The application of science to practice is usually made possible only by slow and arduous *cumulation* of findings over long periods of time. Literally millions of man-hours of research precede the current practical applications of a science like physics. There is certainly no reason to suppose that any less work will be required to reach comparable levels of applicability of social science.

Many of the findings from research on intergroup relations will have their chief practical value not so much in specific predictions and immediate action-prescriptions as in the gradual development of basic perspectives and general orientations. Although the social consequences at this level will not be so obvious as in the case of immediate concrete results, their long-run weight may be more important. Immediate prophecy and control may be beyond our grasp in many current problems of social action. Yet the possibilities in this direction are not all negative, as attested by knowledge already accumulated.

Where research does not provide an unequivocal basis for positive prediction, it still offers at least two extremely important possibilities for contributing to understanding and action. First, there is much to be gained from demonstration of the sheer range of possible actions and their accompaniments and consequences. If a particular propaganda effort were made on the assumption that certain effects would be obtained, research on the problem might well find the situation recalcitrant to any positive prediction in the mode of "If you do A, then B and only B will follow." It might be possible, however, to demonstrate a whole series of unanticipated effects; careful study might show not only effect B (say, greater awareness of admirable qualities in a minority group), but also effect C (enhanced fear of competition), effect D (greater awareness of intergroup cultural differences), and so on. Precisely this sort of demonstration may be of inestimable value to practitioners in evaluating alternate possibilities of action. Second, there is the possibility of what may be called negative prediction. Generalizations in this mode will be in such forms as "Under these conditions, X will *not* appear," or "This action will not have as one of its effects . . .," or "This action is impossible because of factors X, Y, and Z in the situation." If research in certain instances can do no more than state the probable limits of particular types of programs or specify the results definitely not to be anticipated, it will have performed a socially vital function in diverting effort away from blind alleys and from the attempt to fulfill wishful but erroneous anticipation.

Finally, in focusing upon purposive "techniques" or "approaches" for reducing intergroup tensions there is no necessary implication that group hostility is subject to elimination or anything approximating complete control by these methods, within the framework of our present culture and society. It is certainly possible that unplanned and essentially non-controllable features of modern society make a relatively high level of intergroup hostility unavoidable.[1] This is a question less likely to be answered by empirical research than by the larger developments of the times. However, hostility and conflict are not either present or completely absent but manifest a wide range of variation and, consequently, purposive attempts at control must be evaluated in terms of resulting increases or decreases rather than presence or absence. This monograph has tried to document the fact that there are specific problems which lend themselves to research testing. It is submitted that the potential results hold considerable promise for scientific advance and social integration.

[1] There are several expressions of this point of view in the symposium edited by L. Bryson and others, *Approaches to National Unity, op. cit.;* probably the most explicit statements are those of Pitirim A. Sorokin (pp. 200–206) and Ludwig Mises (especially p. 160).

APPENDIX

RESEARCH APPROACHES AND TECHNIQUES

Basic Approaches

We begin with a truism. The basic method for arriving at all empirical knowledge is observation, and this remains true no matter how refined the observations, how complicated the means utilized, how elaborate the control of conditions, or how subtle the logic of analysis. In the case of human behavior two broad classes of data may be observed: these are roughly indicated by the phrases "what people say" and "what people do." All else is a matter of definition and inference. No one has ever "seen" a prejudice any more than it is possible to "point to" a mathematical vector. When we are asked how we know that a given individual is "prejudiced against Negroes" there is only one meaningful answer: we have seen him act in certain ways or make certain verbalizations toward or about Negroes or corresponding symbols.

Beyond this point the real difficulties begin.[1] The enormous literature dealing with the general problems of defining variables, obtaining reliable and valid measurements, designing strategic experiments and comparisons, and making inferences from the results is testimony concerning the range and complexity of basic methodological problems. In principle at least, research on intergroup relations involves the same problems—which have the same adequate solutions—as research in other fields; but in actual practice, certain broad questions concerning methods recur with particular persistency. A brief examination of these questions may be in order, therefore, before considering specific research techniques.

The classic type of scientific observation is the pure or controlled experiment in which effects are determined by varying one factor at a time under rigidly controlled conditions.[2] The logical model is simple, and when an ideal design is attained the results are definitive; but the perfect experiment is always difficult and rarely accomplished in any field. For many problems of the social and biological sciences, pure experiments are impossible. In the study of intergroup relations only limited

[1] That is, so far as the practical problems of empirical study are concerned; various philosophical problems and related broader "methodological" questions need not detain us here.

[2] It should not be overlooked that certain important natural sciences cannot use experimentation at all, or can practice it to only a limited extent, e.g., geology, astronomy, and some fields of biological science.

approximations to the ideal design can be expected. There are, however, some situations in which rather rigorous controls are possible. Thus, there are many formally organized groups under more or less authoritative control in which it is possible to vary the stimulus systematically while keeping a number of relevant conditions constant. In certain school and church programs, military organizations, work situations, and various kinds of "institutions" this will be feasible on occasion. Probably the most obvious example of this type of study is the before-and-after testing [3] of matched experimental and control classes in schools when one variable in the instruction is deliberately varied.

In the rare cases in which nearly "pure" experiments can be carried out, the findings will have the virtue of precision, and the causal inferences may be unequivocal. Great as these advantages are, they are accompanied by certain costs. Populations accessible for such experiments usually differ in important respects from other larger populations to which one may wish to apply the generalizations. Second, the very precision—for which we may often read "artificiality"—of the experiment limits wider applicability of the findings. From a long-run scientific viewpoint this may not be a defect, but in relation to immediate action requirements it is often a handicap. In actual social life things do not occur as single factors, but as parts of clusters or patterns. There are, in other words, typical and recurrent intercorrelations of events, often of great complexity, which are quite recalcitrant to laboratory duplication.

There are, however, other "experiments" besides the pure controlled experiment. We shall limit discussion to the ex post facto experiment,[4] because of its particular suitability for the kinds of problems under consideration here. In its most usual design this type of experiment employs schemes of control for comparing two simultaneously existing instances. It does not set up the experimental conditions beforehand, but utilizes "natural" happenings and introduces its controls after the fact through selection of cases and symbolic manipulation of variables. It may work from causes to effects, or from effects to causes. In either case the research operations approach the status of experiment to the extent that control of factors is achieved.

The details of the study design and the difficulties in control need

---

[3] Adequate results can sometimes be obtained with a single ("after") measurement. This is greatly dependent, however, upon the closeness of the matching of control and experimental groups, and is not the preferred design whenever the more comprehensive testing is possible.

[4] A concise treatment of the varieties of experiment in social science is given by Ernest Greenwood, *Experimental Sociology: A Study in Method* (New York: Kings Crown Press, 1945). The present discussion draws heavily upon this work.

not be treated here. One specific illustration, however, will suggest the central elements in the ex post facto experiment. Suppose that in similar areas of the same city there are two public housing developments, one of which is bi-racial while the other practices racial segregation. The two projects have been established for a period of three years. The original white applicants for the houses did not know, at the time of application, of the nonsegregated character of the one development; and selective applications or transfers to the other project were disallowed on technical grounds. An acute housing shortage created strong pressure to accept the conditions as laid down. Records of the housing agency make it possible to locate all applicants, including those who have moved out after spending a time in the development. About 6,000 families are available for study.

We wish to determine the effects of living under nonsegregated conditions upon the opinions and behavior of the white residents. Assume that adequate techniques of observation and measurement are available or can be contrived. The ex post facto experiment then consists in securing such control over relevant factors that differences between persons who have lived or are living in the two projects can safely be imputed to the one variable of segregation or nonsegregation. In this case it is possible to match groups of families with respect to region of previous residence, educational level, rural-urban origin, occupational status, age of family head, religion, national stock, and certain indices of previous associations with Negroes. Other factors may be controlled insofar as this proves feasible. Matching of individual families on the first few variables may so rapidly deplete the groups as to necessitate resort to equation of the frequency distributions on the remaining factors. Let us assume, however, that it is possible eventually to derive groups which are homogeneous with respect to the selected control-factors, but differ in their interracial housing experience.[5] We then observe the relevant attitudes and behavior of the respective groups. To the degree that significant differences are found we will be justified in concluding that interracial housing does or does not have specified effects.

Examples of the procedure could be multiplied to show its numerous variations, some of its difficulties, and the range of its potential application.[6] In the interests of brevity, however, the summary opinion may be given that discriminating and careful use of this design holds con-

---

[5] To have adequate control, it would of course be necessary to include not only present residents but also those who have withdrawn their applications or who have dropped out of the two projects.

[6] This has been done in some detail by Greenwood, *op. cit.*

siderable promise as a basic method for research on the effects of action-programs affecting intergroup relations. Certain analogues in techniques of partial correlation and the analysis of variance are applicable to the data resulting from the remaining types of study to be discussed.

The third method of approach, in order of decreasing rigor, consists in comparison of concrete cases without the precise control of individual factors found in experimental designs. This is the "natural comparison" or "uncontrolled experiment" which, for one thing, is of such prime importance in suggesting hypotheses and isolating variables. Insofar as the selection of cases for comparison is based on careful equating of factors, it shades over into the ex post facto experiment. In other instances the groups and situations selected for study may differ in a number of major respects, and there is a corresponding uncertainty in inferring causes and effects. Where this is true, stable inferences are usually dependent upon repetitive, cumulative observations of many cases which represent rotating combinations of factors. Sufficiently numerous and strategic observations may permit detecting the constant and variable, the necessary and the non-essential circumstances. Thus, repeated observations of race riots have built up a list of the specific accompanying conditions which appear to be universally present in such outbreaks and which are not found when riots do not occur. There is therefore a strong presumption that at least these factors must be regarded as "causes."

Comparative studies in this general pattern are exceedingly common. Random examples include comparisons of factories employing a mixed labor force with those hiring only majority group members; of communities having different patterns of intergroup relations; of schools using different techniques of intercultural education; and of communities presumably affected and unaffected by certain types of intergroup programs. The comparison of selected "cases" on a broad scale is well illustrated in the work of certain historians (e.g., Teggart, Toynbee). Anthropologists have made a number of comparisons between total cultures (e.g., Mead, Benedict). Practitioners in intergroup programs have relied heavily upon relatively unsystematic comparisons of total situations and programs.

Finally, we have a number of studies which are restricted to descriptive inventories or to the measurement of trends. Here belong all the cross-sectional surveys which simply index intergroup opinions and behaviors as of a given time, as well as those which report readings for successive periods. These data are merely the raw materials for establishing relationships and determining probabilities, and these studies do not represent a separate method of research so much as failure to carry out one of the strategic approaches just outlined. When studies are set up in this way they exclude the possibility of direct comparisons between situations selected to control complicating factors. Any comparisons made are on a relatively crude and "opportunistic" basis, as for example, relating a change in mass attitudes to a war, depression, or other specific event, or comparing the attitudes of broad economic classes in the population. There have been and probably will be many instances in which our only recourse is to what Max Weber called the "mental experiment"; i.e., lacking empirical control of variables, we are forced to rely upon logical control by "thinking away" one factor at a time in order to arrive at causal imputations. Although this is always a hazardous undertaking, it will sometimes be the only possible procedure, and by means of it mature and highly trained scholars have obtained useful and important results.

In general, *if all other things are equal,* a study is the better the more closely it approaches the design of the pure experiment. But practical limitations are such that most really important problems—both socially and scientifically speaking—would go by default were research always held to its most rigorous model. Furthermore, precision and rigor are not ends in themselves but are relative to the needs confronted in any particular case; many of our current requirements can be adequately met by skillful use of comparative methods, short of ideal experimental conditions.[7]

We have not yet referred to certain methodological questions often discussed as basic, such as case studies vs. statistical methods, or, "attitude studies" as contrasted with analyses of "behavior." These important questions are legitimately considered within the field of specific techniques of research, to which we now turn our attention.

Specific Research Techniques

General considerations. Just as the promise of a study is dependent upon its basic design, so the findings rest upon the adequacy of the specific research techniques utilized. Central questions, therefore, are:

[7] It should be noted that the search for "causes" and "effects" is not the only legitimate approach to scientific problems. Much of physiological research, for example, consists of determining the conditions necessary to maintain a certain state of organic equilibrium, and of analyzing the mutual interrelations of variables which determine a given condition of bodily functioning. There apparently are many social problems to which an analogous type of thinking is applicable.

What are the available tools? What are the grestest needs? Our appraisal will be made easier by reviewing a few preliminary considerations.

In the forefront of discussion about research techniques for the study of intergroup relations are a number of hallowed questions concerning "attitude" study. Research in this field stands to gain much by a shift in emphasis away from too exclusive preoccupation with what people say, especially in responses on paper and pencil tests. This does not imply that one is justified in categorizing them as "mere verbalizations" in contrast to "actual behavior" which is supposed somehow to be more "real." [8] A large part of all human behavior is verbal—certainly in intergroup matters—and the extent of its future control will depend upon what is learned about it. It is known that people often make statements which are sharply at variance with things they do, and these very "discrepancies" frequently turn out to be important and revealing.

In the area of action dealing with group tensions the problem appears in an implicit assumption that a change in attitudes will bring some correlated change in other behavior. Unless verbalizations in situations unlike those of daily living are valued for their own sake, there is no rationale for the attention directed toward changes in expressions of opinion. From ordinary observation as well as from extensive research and clinical experience it is clear that what people say is sometimes consistent with their other actions, but the two often diverge widely and are sometimes in direct opposition. Both theoretical expectations and research findings suggest that interracial and intercultural behavior is peculiarly subject to discrepancies of avowal and practice. Prejudice is, by definition, something which people are disposed to conceal or obscure under some circumstances. This is especially evident when a person holding hostile attitudes is aware that his prejudices conflict with values or principles to which he is nominally committed, or which are accepted in his society. Conversely, a current stereotype may be given lip service, while actual behavior toward persons so labeled may not correspond to the verbal blueprint. It has been suggested that Southerners "treat Negroes better" than they talk about them, while Northerners' verbalizations may be more favorable than their usual behavior.[9] LaPiere

[8] This caution is pertinent: "Neither overt behaviour nor opinion [or verbal behaviour] can be regarded as a perfectly reliable indicator of the underlying attitude . . . It is important to bear in mind that a man's behaviour may be as deceitful as his language . . . there is no reason why preference should be given to the one rather than to the other as a means of determining his attitude." (I. D. MacCrone, *Race Attitudes in South Africa*, London: Oxford University Press, 1937, p. 146.) For a concise discussion of this issue see G. A. Lundberg, *Social Research* (New York: Longmans, Green and Co., 1929), pp. 201–203.
[9] Robert K. Merton, "Fact and Factitiousness in Ethnic Opinionnaires," *American Sociological Review*, 5:13–28 (1940).

has reported an instance of an unfavorable stereotype which was not acted upon in the relevant field of behavior.[10] It is known that in interviews containing items about Negroes or Jews different results are obtained with interviewers who are identifiable as members or nonmembers of the respective groups.[11]

Thus, intergroup relations are especially likely to involve discrepancies between opinion and other behavior and between publicly expressed and privately held attitudes. Meanwhile, a vast number of investigations deal only with verbalizations. One of the most pressing needs is for studies which will grasp and reveal relations between verbalizations and other social actions, and will specify in considerable detail the agreement or lack of agreement between responses obtained through questionnaires or interviews and responses evoked by various types of "real" situations. This is usually posed as the problem of validation in attitude and opinion studies. Actually, this may be regarded as unfortunate phrasing. Do we validate measurement of people's opinions by reference to their overt behavior (verbal or nonverbal) outside of the test situation? And do we then validate our observations of this behavior by reference to the test results? Instead of looking at the problem in this light it may be more fruitful to argue that the validity of each of these sets of observations is a separate problem.[12] Rather than concern over which is valid and in what degree, the question in terms of research technique is: How can it be determined what research observations are most predictive of the subjects' other relevant behaviors? [13]

This simple recasting of the problem results in detailed questions suitable for direct testing. Of every research instrument we then ask whether it produces results which adequately reflect, i.e., are usefully correlated with, whatever behavior we are interested in predicting from the findings. If the instrument is an attitude scale, it may be found highly predictive of certain kinds of verbalizations in some contexts, but far

[10] R. T. LaPiere, "Attitudes vs. Actions," Social Forces, 13:230–237 (1934).

[11] Hadley Cantril, Gauging Public Opinion (Princeton: Princeton University Press, 1944); unpublished experiments of the Research Branch, Information and Education Division, U. S. War Department; Duane Robinson and Sylvia Rohde, "Two Experiments with an Anti-Semitism Poll," Journal of Abnormal and Social Psychology, 41:136–144 (1946).

[12] The validity of an item can be shown to depend ultimately upon logical consistency with concepts (propositions, scientific theorems) already laid down. See Raymond V. Bowers, "Discussion: An Analysis of the Problem of Validity," American Sociological Review, 1:69–74 (1936).

[13] Compare this statement: "It is not simply a question of whether or not overt behavior 'coincides' with expressed or endorsed opinions. This way of formulating the problem obscures one of its basic aspects, namely, may we assume the amount and direction of spread between opinion and action to be relatively constant for different groups?" (Robert K. Merton, op. cit., p. 21)

less dependable for forecasting other actions of interest. If the research aim is to predict from scale scores what people will say or write in specified contexts, then to the degree that this can be done the scale is measuring what it is supposed to measure. It is quite another matter, however, to draw any conclusions from the hypothetical case in which this can be done as to the efficiency of the scale scores in predicting other behaviors. The latter in its turn must be established by empirical test.

Any kind of attitude test (or interview guide, etc.) is used in the first place because of presumed advantages in precision and economy. If well constructed, the test will make possible a more precise classification or ranking of individuals or groups than could be derived from less systematic procedures. Aside from ease of manipulation of the resulting data, the great potential economy in using test techniques is that they may reduce the need for direct observation of spontaneous behavior, which is enormously expensive and time consuming. Yet this potential advantage becomes actual only to the extent that the test results make it possible to predict this behavior, under specified conditions. In spite of the hundreds of opinion and attitude studies now accumulated, very little has been done to relate behavior in the test situation to behavior out of it. What does a given score on a scale labeled "attitude toward the Negro" signify in terms of a range of behaviors like the following: organizing or taking part in a riot or lynching; refusing employment; ordering out of a restaurant; accepting as a co-worker; entertaining in one's home? Such patterns of behavior are concrete objects of interest to all those who work to change or maintain existing patterns of inter-group relations. Presumably, measurements other than those made from direct observation of such uncontrolled activities are of interest in the field of social action only insofar as the indirect measurements are pre-dictive of the behavior which is the object of concern. All this seems trite, but the necessary testing of research instruments largely remains to be done. Until it is done we continually face the necessity of making strained and problematical inferences from research results to the situation of action, and vice versa.

Correlation of attitude measurements with directly observed behavior is not, of course, the only way in which the basis of inference can be strengthened.[14] A common technique is to compare the results from a particular test given to two or more groups known to differ in behavior, as evidenced for example by activity in certain organizations. A variant

[14] Cf. Q. McNemar, "Opinion-Attitude Methodology," *Psychological Bulletin*, 43:296–297 (1946).

of this procedure is to compare groups which are expected to differ because of the presence of circumstances known to be correlated closely with differences in attitude. Some studies have relied upon the ratings of close acquaintances, teachers, etc. Intensive interviewing offers considerable help.

In summary: (1) there is need for greater emphasis upon observation of total behavior, not just verbal test results; (2) there is need for relating verbal to nonverbal, and test to nontest behavior.

Actually, the discussion has already implied another point of considerable importance: the need for research to keep close to real life situations. This will remain a requisite for the best research, even that done under rigorously controlled "laboratory" conditions. Direct observation of spontaneous behavior can serve in the first instance as a source of hypotheses for testing. It is of importance also in devising test situations, wording questions, and planning other details of data collection. Further, it provides a wider context for the interpretation of specific research findings, perhaps especially for those drawn from limited populations or based upon responses elicited under simplified controlled conditions. In the latter function direct observation frequently suggests the presence of factors, not previously taken into account, which may obscure, warp, or otherwise complicate the predicted processes and relationships in the action situation. Furthermore, there are some types of problems and circumstances in which direct observation must be a major research approach, as in the case of rare or large-scale events such as riots, and in certain subtle and continuing processes such as changes in the detailed intergroup etiquette of a local community.

Only passing reference need be made to the general problems in the use of statistical methods in social research, since they have been so extensively treated elsewhere and since statistical facility is now nominally a part of standard research equipment. Certain specific problems, e.g., attitude scaling, will be touched upon below. The most important general points concern problems of sampling and of testing the significance of differences. Modern sampling theory and methods are adequate for the great majority of studies which have been made or proposed in this field. The three pitfalls which are still common enough to warrant continuous caution are: (1) overgeneralization from biased samples, i.e., those subject to systematic, noncompensating error; (2) conclusions drawn from inadequate samples, those which are too small for satisfactory levels of sampling error in totals or subgroups; (3) use of uneconomical samples, those which fail to secure the maximum number of cases and maximum representativeness with least effort, time, and cost. Examples of studies adequate with respect to these sampling characteristics stand out against many failures.

With respect to the significance of differences, it is not desirable here to go into the detailed statistical problems, except to stress two points which are particularly important for all studies using controlled comparisons. Whenever changes in matched groups are being compared the tests of reliability to be applied are those which take into account the correlation between measurements on the respective groups.[15] To do otherwise is to overestimate the sampling error; this will lead in some instances to the conclusion that no reliable differences exist when in fact there are real differences. It is true that differences so small as to be obscured by use of formulae lacking the correlational terms may be of little practical importance in many cases, but this is not always so. In testing the effects of specific propaganda stimuli, for example, the measurable effects are ordinarily quite small; yet the discovery of even a very small difference between alternative techniques may be of great practical importance inasmuch as the particular technique may be repeatedly applied to large populations over a period of time. To dismiss a small difference, on grounds of a misplaced statistical application, might then lead to unnecessary errors in action programs. Similar implications derive from the second point, i.e., the requirement that the significance of net changes in comparison groups must be tested rather than that of the change in an "experimental" group only. It is the *difference* between the changes in group A and in group B which most strictly demonstrates whether or not a reliable change has been produced.[16]

Available techniques. The techniques in most common use are adequate for certain limited problems, but are not fully satisfactory for testing many of the more important hypotheses in the field. Nevertheless, much significant work can be done and has already been done with present tools. The available techniques may be classified according to the four main functions served by research techniques:

I. *Collecting data*
 1. Direct observation of spontaneous behavior without instigation by the observer

[15] This point is emphasized in standard statistical works; see, for example, C. C. Peters and W. R. VanVoorhis, *Statistical Procedures and Their Mathematical Bases* (New York: McGraw-Hill Book Company, 1940), Chapter XVI, "The Technique of Controlled Experimentation."
[16] Q. McNemar, *op. cit.*, p. 339.

    2. Sociometric observation and tests
        a. Direct charting of interaction
        b. Verbal choices
    3. Interviewing
        a. "Questionnaire" type: using a standard set of direct questions
        b. "Focused" type
        c. "Nondirective" type
    4. Questionnaires administered to groups
        a. Reporting *opinions*
            (1) General or abstract
            (2) Situational or concrete
        b. Reporting *behavior*
            (1) General
            (2) Specific
    5. Self-written documents: autobiographies, letters, diaries, etc.
    6. Projective tests
    7. Other, "laboratory" tests

II. *Measuring or ranking*
    1. Observational counting and rating of behavior
    2. Interviewer ratings
    3. Self-ratings
    4. Qualitative classification of items, e.g., item responses to questionnaires or interviews, sequences of acts
    5. Scales of opinion

III. *Discovering relationships*
    1. Simple intercorrelation
        a. Cross-tabulation of items
        b. Correlation and contingency coefficients
    2. Complex intercorrelation
        a. Multiple
        b. Partial
        c. Factor analysis

IV. *Safeguarding conclusions*
    1. Statistical indexes of reliability, e.g., test-retest errors, internal consistency
    2. Tests of validity
    3. Tests of significance of differences, e.g., standard error, Chi-square, analysis of variance

Limitations of space preclude discussion of Categories III and IV. The others will be treated in summary fashion only; the references cited cover many considerations which must be omitted here.

For present purposes, the most important comment on the method of *direct observation* is that there are significant unrealized possibilities of developing techniques which may greatly further objectivity, systematization, and quantification. Exploratory work has been done on some of the relevant problems,[17] and further developments should be encouraged. Reliability in the sense of agreement of observers can be increased by development of standard recording forms, precise definition of behavior units to be recorded, and use of careful sampling controls.

Fruitful application of such techniques is of course dependent upon placing observers in those areas and positions in the social structure where the necessary realistic data can be recorded. A difficulty in many past studies has been that observation was restricted to special populations and the observers were often limited to the role of middle class, academic, "outsiders." Both these rather serious limitations have been occasioned in part by the meagerness of research funds, which often has restricted the social scientist to the campus or other local situations. Use of trained participant-observers in strategic roles in community groups and strata presents an opportunity for systematizing representative observations of spontaneous intergroup behavior.

The importance of developments along these lines can hardly be exaggerated. What we call common-sense knowledge is primarily based upon informal, personal observation—often limited and biased in various ways. Yet the value of such knowledge is widely recognized, and more representative and systematic observation may be expected to yield results far more significant than those achieved up to now. To cite only one example, studies of patterns of segregation have shown many instances in which the dominant ideology is clear-cut, but in which actual

[17] Dorothy S. Thomas, *Some New Techniques for Studying Social Behavior* (New York: Teachers College, Columbia University, 1929); "An Attempt to Develop Precise Measurements in the Social Behavior Field," *Sociologus,* 9:436–456 (1933); studies of E. V. C. Berne reported in G. Murphy, L. B. Murphy and T. M. Newcomb, *Experimental Social Psychology* (New York: Harper & Brothers, 1937), pp. 263–265; W. I. Newstetter, M. J. Feldstein and T. M. Newcomb, *Group Adjustment: A Study in Experimental Sociology* (Cleveland: Western Reserve University Press, 1938); L. J. Carr, "Experimental Sociology: A Preliminary Note on Theory and Method," *Social Forces,* 8:63–74 (1929) and "Experimentation in Face-to-Face Interaction," *American Sociological Society Publications,* 24(2):174–176 (1930). Considerable work on techniques of observation has been done in connection with the research program of the Boy Scouts of America.

practice is complicated, labile, and on occasion markedly at variance with expressed opinions.[18] Further and more systematic observation might turn up important clues as to specific points of resistance and flexibility—clues having immediate bearing upon action programs.

Sociometric observations and tests, developed from the work of J. L. Moreno, have been applied to the study of intergroup relations, especially in school situations.[19] Although not all the claims made for those techniques are likely to be realized, the charting of interpersonal choices is certainly a useful technique in the study of many face-to-face groups. It is well adapted to certain studies of experimentally induced changes as, for example, in before-and-after testing of patterns of personal interaction in school groups which have and have not been exposed to a given program of intercultural education. Parallel applications to work and residential groups should prove feasible in many instances.

Any attempt to give a full treatment of the general problems of *interviewing* lies outside the scope of the present study. However, a few of the major problems and some of the means which have been devised to cope with them should be noted. First, in research on intergroup relations the factor of "interviewer bias" is crucial. Previous studies have demonstrated that the apparent group-membership of the interviewer significantly affects the responses elicited.[20] There is little point in discussing which set of responses—those given to interviewers from one group or the other—are the "real" opinions; which set of data is preferable depends upon the purposes of the investigation. It is essential, however, that the possible differentials be recognized in planning a study and taken into account in interpretation of the findings. Aside from group membership indicated by such criteria as color or name, many less obvious characteristics of interviewers undoubtedly affect results.[21]

[18] Cf. Charles S. Johnson, *Patterns of Negro Segregation* (New York: Harper & Brothers, 1943).

[19] Representative investigations include: J. L. Moreno, *Who Shall Survive* (Washington: Nervous and Mental Disease Publishing Co., 1934); J. H. Criswell, "A Sociometric Study of Race Cleavage in the Classroom," *Archives of Psychology*, No. 235 (1939); E. L. Hartley and A. Mintz, "A Technique for the Study of the Dynamics of the Racial Saturation Point," *Sociometry*, 9:14–20 (1946).

[20] Duane Robinson and Sylvia Rohde, *op. cit.*, and "A Public Opinion Study of Anti-Semitism in New York City," *American Sociological Review*, 10:511–515 (1945); unpublished studies of the Research Branch, Information and Education Division, U. S. War Department, showed that Negro and white interviewers secured different responses from Negro soldiers.

[21] See H. Cantril, *op. cit.*; D. Katz, "Do Interviewers Bias Poll Results?" *Public Opinion Quarterly*, 6:248–268 (1942); T. E. Neely, *A Study of Error in the Interview* (privately published, 1937).

Careful selection of personnel and training in uniform procedures seem the only available methods for minimizing these effects.

A second problem of wide scope concerns the type of interview. Several major variations are possible: (1) In the "questionnaire" interview the respondent is asked a series of prepared questions in a definite order. Respondents may be given a questionnaire to follow during the interview and merely asked to choose among prepared alternative answers to each question, just as in the case of group-administered questionnaires. Or, only the questions may be fixed, and the interviewer records the "free" answers as nearly verbatim as possible. In a variant of this procedure the interviewer asks a memorized list of questions and records the answers after the interview. (2) The "focused" interview, as described by Merton and Kendall, is intermediate between that using a fixed set of questions and the "nondirective" types discussed below.[22] The interviewer has a framework of questions which he wishes to have answered, but he goes on to explore the "reasons" and "motives" which may underlie specific replies, and he allows the respondent freedom to follow up his own chains of associations. The main function of the interviewer is to "focus" attention upon a particular problem or area of interest, rather than to dictate specific questions. Thus a focused interview would not permit the conversation to ramble over any variety of topics; on the other hand, once the discussion is focused on a broad area, care is taken to avoid imposing a particular frame of reference upon the respondent.

The "nondirective" interview is one in which the interviewer simply broaches a given topic or takes a subject chosen by the interviewee and then tries to encourage him to talk under a minimum of direct questioning or guidance.[23] A number of specific techniques have been developed to insure the nondirectional quality of the interviewer's role, e.g., repeating the respondent's last comment, allowing silences, giving

[22] Robert K. Merton and Patricia L. Kendall, "The Focused Interview," *American Journal of Sociology*, 51:541–557 (1946).

The "open-end" questioning advocated by Rensis Likert has some characteristics of both "questionnaire" and "focused" interviewing. See H. E. Skott, "Attitude Research in the Department of Agriculture," *Public Opinion Quarterly*, 7:280–292 (1943); Q. McNemar, *op. cit.*, pp. 319–321, and references cited there; P. F. Lazarsfeld, "The Controversy over Detailed Interviews—An Offer for Negotiation," *Public Opinion Quarterly*, 8:38–60 (1944); H. C. Link, "An Experiment in Depth Interviewing on the Issue of Internationalism vs. Isolationism," *Public Opinion Quarterly*, 7:267–279 (1943).

[23] The term "nondirectional" has received currency from Carl Rogers. Cf. his "The Nondirective Method as a Technique for Social Research," *American Journal of Sociology*, 50:279–283 (1945)

noncommittal responses, turning questions back to the respondent, and so on.[24] Such interviews are time consuming and require considerable skill, and it is difficult to objectify the resulting data. For these reasons they will seldom be practicable as the sole source of information in large-scale studies. On the other hand, the intensive nondirective interview in skilled hands can produce very important insights and detailed qualitative description. Its primary value thus lies in its usefulness as a supplement and check upon results obtained by less intensive and more nearly "formalized" techniques.

Some type of interviewing is essential to nearly all studies of intergroup relations. Even if other techniques are relied upon for the main bodies of data, interviewing is always a desirable supplement. In questionnaire studies extensive pretest interviewing is almost always required, to formulate relevant questions in appropriate language and form.[25] This step often requires considerable time and effort but its omission usually means an inadequate questionnaire. This function of the interview is really part of the more general process of suggesting and formulating hypotheses. Further, the interview is unexcelled as a source of materials describing complex opinions, revealing sequences and associations of thoughts and feelings, and uncovering implicit assumptions and other "depth" aspects of attitudes. In all studies which rely on polling, questionnaires, and the like, it is highly desirable that a sample of respondents be followed up with intensive interviews.

Administration of questionnaires or other paper and pencil tests *to groups* is the technique in most common use for studying intergroup attitudes. A large number of such tests have been developed, and will be discussed further in connection with problems of measurement.

Questionnaires may ask for expressions of opinion, either general or specific, or for accounts of behavior. The best example of asking for a highly generalized type of opinion is furnished by the Bogardus test of social distance.[26] Respondents are asked to indicate whether they will accept members of different groups (taken as wholes) in varying degrees of closeness of relationship; they are asked specifically to think in general terms, not of the best or the worst members of each category. At the opposite extreme from such generalized questions are the multitudes

[24] Some worth-while suggestions are given by F. J. Roethlisberger, *Management and Morale* (Cambridge: Harvard University Press, 1941).

[25] Cf. the statement of McNemar, *op. cit.,* p. 329.

[26] The development of the method is traced in three articles by Emory S. Bogardus: "Measuring Social Distance," *Journal of Applied Sociology,* 9:299–308 (1925); "Social Distance and Its Origins," *ibid.,* pp. 216–226; "A Social Distance Scale," *Sociology and Social Research,* 17:265–271 (1933).

of specific questions on opinions. A special development of the specific-question approach is the use of descriptions of particular *situations* as stimuli for responses. Relevant illustrations are the studies by Rosander, Harlan, and Pace.[27] The questionnaire used by Rosander explored responses toward several types of social situations, including Negro-white contacts. He suggests that not only verbal descriptions of situations but also various visual stimuli could be used as objects of questioning. Harlan presented twelve situations involving Jew-Gentile relations and asked his respondents to approve or disapprove of the actions described. The test developed by Pace includes intergroup contact as part of a series of situations.

Questionnaire studies have also asked respondents to report on their own past experiences and behavior, as illustrated in the recent work of Allport and Kramer and in the earlier study of Ford.[28]

Self-written documents of various kinds relevant to intergroup problems have been used chiefly as teaching aids and illustrative documentation rather than as material for research. In the field of personality study their advantages and disadvantages have been fairly well explored.[29] As a source of data on "objective" past happenings they are subject to multiple distortions through selective forgetting and the like. They are often difficult to collect and interpret, and are not well suited to provide evidence on experimentally induced changes. With all their disadvantages, however, personal documents have some of the virtues of the interview in suggesting hypotheses and providing a whole picture of complex attitudes and sequences. For this reason, if for no other, they will continue to have a place in the total scheme of research.

A variety of possible tests are included under the rubric of *projective* techniques. The definitive characteristic of all projective tests is the presentation of a relatively unstructured (ambiguous) stimulus or situation to which the subject responds, usually in a "free" fashion. All uses of the technique rely upon the tendency of people to interpret un-

[27] A. C. Rosander, "An Attitude Scale Based upon Behavior Situations," *Journal of Social Psychology*, 8:3–15 (1937); Howard H. Harlan, "Some Factors Affecting Attitude toward Jews," *American Sociological Review*, 7:816–827 (1942); C. R. Pace, "A Situations Test to Measure Social-Political-Economic Attitudes," *Journal of Social Psychology*, 10:331–344 (1939).

[28] G. W. Allport and B. M. Kramer, "Some Roots of Prejudice," *Journal of Psychology*, 22:9–39 (1946); Robert N. Ford, "Scaling Experience by a Multiple-Response Technique: A Study of White-Negro Contacts," *American Sociological Review*, 6:9–23 (1941).

[29] For a general evaluation see G. W. Allport, *The Use of Personal Documents in Psychological Science*, Social Science Research Council Bulletin 49 (New York, 1942). Some of the guiding principles for collection and analysis of such documents as used in life-history studies are set forth in John Dollard, *Criteria for the Life History* (New Haven: Yale University Press, 1935).

structured or ambiguous stimuli in terms of their own major psychological needs and dominant frames of reference. Lacking a definitive perceptual frame in the stimulus itself, the individual is likely to project his own conscious or unconscious wants and stereotypes into the material presented. The main development of the technique has occurred in connection with studies of personality.[30] Probably the best known projective test is the Rorschach, which utilizes a series of ambiguous inkblots into which subjects read their own interpretations.[31] Complex methods of scoring and diagnosis have been evolved, and lively controversy exists as to the reliability and validity of these methods. The Murray Thematic Apperception Test[32] consists of a series of pictures about which respondents are asked to write brief descriptions or stories. An adaptation of this technique for the study of intergroup relations has recently been proposed, but research findings are not yet available. It is proposed "to investigate the mechanism of social attitudes by means of a visual projective test . . . *a series of pictures dealing with all areas of social interaction* with particular emphasis on intergroup relations, such as Negro-white and Jew-Christian relationships." [33] An earlier study by Proshansky used a series of ambiguous pictures to investigate attitudes toward labor.[34] Pictures of labor situations were intermingled with unrelated items. Subjects were instructed to write for two and one-half minutes on what they thought each slide represented, after viewing it for five seconds.

A somewhat different but related technique has been used by Morgan to investigate attitudes toward the Japanese.[35] His method, which appears less widely applicable than projective techniques proper, is to present a

[30] L. K. Frank, "Projective Methods for the Study of Personality," *Journal of Psychology*, 8:389–413 (1939); P. M. Symonds and E. A. Samuel, "Projective Methods in the Study of Personality," *Review of Educational Research*, 11:80–93 (1941).

[31] The applicability of this technique to problems of intergroup relations remains unknown. For its uses in general personality diagnosis, the following are among the best known expositions: S. J. Beck, *Rorschach's Test* and *Rorschach's Test: II. A Variety of Personality Pictures* (New York: Grune and Stratton, 1944, 1945); Ruth Bachner and Florence Halpern, *The Clinical Application of the Rorschach Test* (New York: Grune and Stratton, 1942); Bruno Klopfer and Douglas M. Kelly, *The Rorschach Technique* (Yonkers-on-Hudson: World Book Company, 1942).

[32] H. A. Murray and others, *Explorations in Personality* (New York: Oxford University Press, 1938).

[33] Henry Loeblowitz-Lennard and Frank Riessman, Jr., "A Preliminary Report on a Social Perception Test: A New Approach to Attitude Research," *Social Forces*, 24:423–427 (1946).

[34] H. M. Proshansky, "A Projective Method for the Study of Attitudes," *Journal of Abnormal and Social Psychology*, 38:393–395 (1943).

[35] J. J. B. Morgan, "Attitudes of Students toward the Japanese," *Journal of Social Psychology*, 21:219–227 (1945).

series of syllogisms accompanied by a check-list of prepared "solutions." In some instances none of the multiple-choice categories can be derived by syllogistic reasoning. Deviations from strictly logical reasoning are then interpreted as distortions occasioned by the influence of under-lying opinions. This technique probably has only limited application to relatively well educated and articulate groups.

Techniques of *measurement and ranking* other than scaling require only brief comment. In the first place, we may count units of behavior and rate them as to variation in favorableness, intensity, and so on. The problems of definition of variables and of observer reliability have already been mentioned. Second, we may secure ratings by interviewers, close acquaintances, or the respondents themselves. In spite of the seeming subjectivity of such ratings, various studies have indicated fairly high reliabilities, and in some instances have shown correlations with standard scales as high as the intercorrelations of some of the scales.[36] The relation of results obtained by scaling to those found by rating schemes warrants further exploration.

Attitude scales have been classified by Rose according to five types of basic techniques:[37] those attributed to Bogardus, Thurstone, Likert, Sletto, and Guttman. All these methods have been so widely discussed and applied that we need only to cite some of the applications and note major advantages and disadvantages.

The Bogardus "scale" is essentially a method of ranking groups and does not provide for equidistant scale intervals. It is a rigid technique in the sense of being applicable only to a narrow range of problems, and is not productive of data on complex dimensions of opinion. However, it is simple to construct and administer and has some utility as a rough way of ranking groups according to reactions to stereotypes.

Thurstone's method of scaling has been more widely used than any other in studies of intergroup attitudes.[38] The technique is laborious,

[36] Cf. B. L. Riker, "A Comparison of Methods Used in Attitude Research," *Journal of Abnormal and Social Psychology*, 39:24–42 (1944), and "Comparison of Attitude Scales— A Correction," *ibid.*, 40:102–103 (1945); T. N. Ewing, "A Study of Certain Factors Involved in Changes of Opinion," *Journal of Social Psychology*, 16:63–68 (1942).

[37] Arnold Rose, *Studies in Reduction of Prejudice* (Chicago: American Council on Race Relations, 1947). It is unnecessary here to duplicate the description of these techniques presented in that monograph.

[38] Basic publications by L. L. Thurstone include: "The Method of Paired Comparisons for Social Values," *Journal of Abnormal and Social Psychology*, 21:384–400 (1927); "An Experimental Study of Nationality Preferences," *Journal of General Psychology*, 1:405–425 (1928); "Attitudes Can Be Measured," *American Journal of Sociology*, 33:529–554 (1928); and with E. J. Chave, *The Measurement of Attitude* (Chicago: University of Chicago Press, 1929).

involving these steps: (1) collection of a large number of statements (usually 100 or more) representing a wide range of possible attitudes; (2) ranking of the statements in 11 classes according to favorableness-unfavorableness by a large number of "judges," ideally at least 100; (3) determination of scale values (the median rank of each statement); (4) elimination of ambiguous, irrelevant, and nondiscriminating items; (5) selection of items to give an even distribution over the range of scale values; (6) testing reliability and, in the ideal case, validity as indicated by the known-groups test or some other outside criterion.

A number of Thurstone-type scales have been constructed for measuring intergroup attitudes. The original series prepared at the University of Chicago included scales on attitudes toward the Negro and the Chinese.[39] I. D. MacCrone prepared a scale of attitudes toward natives in South Africa, which has been adapted to the study of attitudes toward the Negro in this country.[40] The technique has been used to construct scales of Negroes' attitudes toward whites and of majority attitudes toward Japanese Americans.[41] The Hinckley scale of attitudes toward the Negro has been applied by several investigators including Smith, Bolton, and Ford.[42] Their studies show that Forms A and B are not strictly comparable and that Form B elicits responses weighted toward a more "unfavorable" position than Form A. Since in before-and-after testing Form A is usually given first and Form B is given after the experimental stimulus, the result of this defect in the scale is to attenuate or obscure actual changes in attitude which may have occurred.

The Thurstone method has recently encountered a number of criticisms.[43] The more important may be summarized as follows: (1) It does not really produce a linear scale: the scores are averages of specific items,

[39] The scale of attitudes toward the Negro, developed by E. D. Hinckley, has A and B Forms which were intended to be comparable. The scale on attitudes toward the Chinese was devised by Ruth Peterson. Both are presented in *Motion Pictures and the Social Attitudes of Children* (New York: The Macmillan Company, 1933) by Ruth Peterson and L. L. Thurstone.

[40] I. D. MacCrone, *op. cit.*, and R. K. Merton, *op. cit.*

[41] E. S. Marks, "Standardization of a Race Attitude Test for Negro Youth," *Journal of Social Psychology*, 18:245–278 (1943); Gwynne Nettler and Elizabeth H. Golding, "The Measurement of Attitudes toward the Japanese in America," *American Journal of Sociology*, 52:31–39 (1946).

[42] Robert N. Ford, *op. cit.*; F. Tredwell Smith, *An Experiment in Modifying Attitudes toward the Negro* (New York: Teachers College, Columbia University, 1943); E. B. Bolton, "Measuring Specific Attitudes toward the Social Rights of the Negro," *Journal of Abnormal and Social Psychology*, 31:384–397 (1937).

[43] Representative sources: Q. McNemar, *op. cit.*, pp. 301–308; R. K. Merton, *op. cit.*; C. Kirkpatrick and S. Stone, "Attitude Measurement and the Comparison of Generations," *Journal of Applied Psychology*, 19:564–582 (1935); C. Kirkpatrick, "Assumptions and Methods in Attitude Measurements," *American Sociological Review*, 1:75–88 (1936).

and there is no guarantee that endorsement of an extreme item means endorsement of the less extreme items which the condition of linearity would require. (2) Scores are biased in the sense that, e.g., a respondent can get a lower prejudice score by checking *many* "anti" statements than by checking only a few of the items supposedly measuring prejudice. (3) The scores on different scales are not directly comparable. (4) The scales involve more than one dimension of opinion; hence, scores are ambiguous because of varying motives inducing the same formal response. (5) The scales are likely to be misleading, when taken alone, through their omission of important complex opinions. The argument is that nondiscriminating statements, eliminated from the scales because of high Q-value, tap opinions which are an essential part of the actual picture.

Although thus criticized, the Thurstone technique retains the feature which largely accounts for its wide popularity: the objectivity of scale values determined by the use of "judges." Except possibly in the rare cases of judges from radically different cultures, the scale values are independent of the personal attitudes of the judges. This is a great advantage, and the rational ranking which it permits is an advance over previous methods.

The chief contender with the Thurstone technique for favor since 1932 has been the approach developed by Likert.[44] After preliminary trials with complicated scoring weights, he found that arbitrary weights of 1 through 5 (attached to response categories ranging from "strongly agree" through "strongly disagree") gave results practically identical with the sigma-unit scoring. Selection of items was made on the basis of internal consistency; each item included was required to be highly correlated with total scores. Results obtained with scales constructed by this method show a satisfactory degree of correlation with those obtained with corresponding Thurstone scales.[45] The scales are easy to understand and simple to construct and apply. A disadvantage of the method is that scale items tend to be concentrated at the extreme values rather than spread evenly over the entire range. McNemar has suggested that a combination of the Thurstone and Likert techniques will remove some of the chief disadvantages of the two taken separately.

Sletto's work represents a development of the criterion of internal consistency already applied by Likert.[46] This "item analysis" requires that each item in the scale measure the same thing as the total scale in the sense that scores on each item are highly correlated with total scores.

None of the techniques so far sketched give any assurance that the items selected to constitute a scale all lie along a single continuum of opinion.[47] This assurance is provided by the technique recently developed by Guttman.[48] The original selection of trial items for his scales is on the same basis as in the other major types of scaling, namely, an a priori judgment that the various statements or questions belong to a common area of opinion. However, the final selection, given the definition of the attitude to be scaled, is objective and unequivocal. Only those items are included which elicit a *pattern* of responses such that endorsement of an extreme item carries with it endorsement of all less extreme items. This means that each scale score has a definite meaning; it represents one and only one combination of responses to all items. If a scale satisfying this condition is found, the items by definition constitute a single variable and the scores distribute the population in a precise rank order. There is no criterion of equality of intervals, but the rankings of different individuals and groups are directly comparable. Scales developed by this technique have been applied to intergroup attitudes of white and Negro soldiers in the U. S. Army,[49] and to the study of intergroup attitudes of college students.[50]

Most of the specific scales now in existence have been constructed by one of the basic methods just outlined. A dubious variant of the Thurstone technique is represented by the "generalized attitude scales" originated by Remmers. A generalized scale to measure attitude toward any group has been published;[51] but the validity of this instrument in

---

[46] E. A. Rundquist and R. F. Sletto, *Personality in the Depression* (Minneapolis: University of Minnesota Press, 1936); R. F. Sletto, *Construction of Personality Scales by the Criterion of Internal Consistency* (Minneapolis: The Sociological Press, 1937). The Likert-Sletto method has been used in the construction of a scale of attitudes toward Jews; see D. J. Levinson and R. N. Sanford, "A Scale for the Measurement of Anti-Semitism," *Journal of Psychology*, 17:339–370 (1944).

[47] At least this is true short of very laborious factor analysis.

[48] Louis Guttman, "A Basis for Scaling Qualitative Data," *American Sociological Review*, 9:139–150 (1944); "A Basis for Analyzing Test-Retest Reliability," *Psychometrika*, 10:255–282 (1945).

[49] To be reported in a forthcoming volume on the work of the Research Branch, Information and Education Division, U. S. War Department, now being prepared under the direction of a committee of the Social Science Research Council.

[50] Unpublished studies of Guttman at Cornell University. Acceptable scales have been developed on attitudes toward Negroes, Jews, and foreigners as well as on various socio-economic issues.

[51] H. H. Grice and H. H. Remmers, *A Scale for Measuring Attitudes toward Races and Nationalities* (LaFayette: Purdue Research Foundation, Purdue University, 1934).

practice has not been demonstrated, although in experiments aimed at modifying attitudes of students it has shown test-retest shifts.[52]

A summary listing of selected studies using scales on intergroup attitudes will suggest the range of application of opinion-ranking instruments already developed:[53]

I. *Thurstone scales:*
>   Rosander (179)
>   Nettler and Golding (156)
>   Droba (58)
>   MacCrone (131)
>   Merton (143)
>   Bolton (20)
>   F. T. Smith (193)
>   Ford (65)
>   Campbell and Stover (30)
>   Manske (132)
>   M. Smith (194)

II. *Bogardus social distance test:*
>   Brooks (26)
>   Dodd (52)
>   Campbell and Stover (30)
>   M. Smith (194)
>   Ford (65)
>   Haag (78)

III. *Likert-Sletto scales:*
>   Levinson and Sanford (117)
>   Allport and Kramer (5)
>   Harlan (80)

IV. *Guttman scales:*
>   Unpublished studies

Needed developments. Before it is possible to establish the effects of forces affecting intergroup relations it is necessary to identify these "effects" and "forces." Further, before it is possible to make any scientific appraisal of the *relative weight* of the factors producing a given result, or of the importance of effects, or of the effectiveness of control techniques, it is necessary to have devices for *measuring or ranking* the

---

[52] H. H. Remmers, "Propaganda in the Schools—Do the Effects Last?", *Public Opinion Quarterly,* 2:197–210 (1938).

[53] Numbers in parentheses refer to items in the Selected Bibliography, pp. 135–145. Studies by the originators of the techniques are included there. In addition to the scales used in these studies, many specific tests have been applied by various students.

relevant variables. In part, therefore, the needs and possibilities in research depend directly upon the techniques of measurement and ranking which exist or can be created on the basis of present insights and experience. Our brief and incomplete review of available techniques leads us to conclude, first, that research of real importance can be done with tools already at hand; but second, that great improvements in technique are needed and that these improvements are possible in the fairly immediate future.

Thus, the first priority is that of developing better instruments of observation and measurement. "Better" means instruments of greater precision, reliability, and validity; it also means techniques of wider applicability than those now in most common use. In listing some of the developments in technique which appear to be most urgently needed, justifications for our recommendations will be held to a minimum in the interests of brevity.

It has already been strongly suggested that one of the prime needs of opinion-attitude studies is the development of validation *in the sense of specifying the relation between verbal-test performances and other relevant behavior*. Nearly all past studies have definitely failed to deal adequately with this problem.[54] The validity of tests and scales must be improved, first, by more careful analysis when the measuring instrument is being constructed of the content of attitude and behavior which is to be indexed, and secondly, by observing the discrimination between individuals and groups which are really known to differ in behavior. The more specific the behavioral criteria, the better; e.g., as against merely showing that a test of attitudes toward Negroes differentiates between "Southerners" and "Northerners," it is preferable to use specific individual behaviors as the criterion.

Insofar as opinions are to be recorded in intergroup studies, one of the important needs is for further development of unidimensional scales of the type originated by Guttman.[55] Where their application is appropriate, such scales have several very great advantages:

(1) They test the hypothesis that a given collection of items can be treated meaningfully as a *single* variable. The result of finding this type of scale is that we work with more homogeneous and precisely defined

---

[54] The only example of a scale on racial attitudes which has been checked against *known* behavior patterns is the test of opinion about Japanese Americans reported by Nettler and Golding, *op. cit.*

[55] See footnote 48, p. 128, *supra*. Cf. also, Ward H. Goodenough, "A Technique for Scale Analysis," *Educational and Psychological Measurement*, 4:179–190 (1944); E. William Noland, "Factors Associated with Absenteeism in a South-Central New York State Industry," unpublished Ph.D. dissertation, Cornell University, 1944.

variables, free from that complex intermingling of several dimensions of opinion which has so often marked conventional tests.

(2) If a scale is found, it is possible to assign individuals to a definite rank-order by means of scores which in the limiting case of a perfect scale reproduce the exact pattern of item responses.

(3) Scale scores provide the most efficient means for predicting any outside criterion. First order correlation of the scores with another variable amounts to multiple correlation of all the individual items with that variable. The advantages in economy of effort alone are obvious.

(4) As over against single items, the scales secure important gains in reliability.

(5) The *relative* character of scale scores is evident and tends to avert the common and fallacious tendency to impute absolute values to item responses. With such scales there is less danger of concluding, for example, that 50 percent of the population is "in favor of" a certain stand just because 50 percent of a sample said "yes" to a particular wording of a single question. There is more likelihood of focusing attention upon "more favorable" or "less favorable" individuals or groups.[56]

There are other advantages in this technique of scaling, especially in statistical manipulation. The most essential feature, however, is that it becomes possible to replace heterogeneous aggregates of items by scales of unambiguous content, permitting precise ranking of individuals along a single continuum.

A point which has received too little attention so far is that the application of the basic technique for constructing this type of scale is in principle not restricted to questionnaires or paper and pencil tests in general. Essentially, scaling is a way of ordering qualitative categories of response; whether the stimuli or responses are verbal or nonverbal is irrelevant. Thus it is entirely conceivable that the test stimuli would consist, not just of direct questions, but of cartoons, pictures, photographs, motion pictures, written materials, drama, "staged" situations, or real events. The responses might consist of checking prepared categories, giving verbal reports, making specific motor movements, or carrying out social acts. The only requirements are *that the responses be categorized,* and *that the categorized responses form the particular graded pattern which defines an acceptable scale.* There are grounds for suspect-

---

[56] This is, of course, a virtue shared by other types of scales, but not by an individual-item approach. The so-called public opinion polls have been conspicuously prone to weakness in converting responses to individual questions into absolute statements of proportions "for" and "against."

ing that verbal test responses are more likely to be scalable than other responses, but this has not been demonstrated.

Even should the nonverbal stimuli-response patterns not be scalable in one dimension, it may still be possible to treat them meaningfully, if less precisely, by methods mentioned hereinafter. A simplified illustration may clarify the possibilities. Suppose that we wish to construct a scale of opinion on certain aspects of Negro-white relations. Let us present a series of staged situations using actual white and Negro actors, or motion pictures of the situations. For each situation we ask the respondent to say whether he approves, disapproves, or is indifferent or undecided toward the depicted behavior in the white (or Negro) roles. The situations would have to be simple and clear; they would be chosen on the hypothesis that they constitute a graded series of difficulty of approval, e.g., ranging from a commercial transaction to an intimate social relationship. We may have 10 situations so distributed that only 10 percent of respondents approve the behavior in situation #1 (most difficult to approve) while 90 percent approve that in situation #10. If the responses form a Guttman scale, the individuals who approve of the first situation will approve the remaining nine in a large proportion of all cases. Similarily, individuals who disapprove of the least difficult item will disapprove of the more difficult ones. Between the two extreme types will be ranged the other respondents who disapprove one or more items, in order of the increasing difficulty of approval demonstrated by the over-all frequencies of response. This would be a perfect or true scale; in various particular series of items only a quasi-scale might appear, that is, a pattern in which one dominant variable is overlaid with essentially random deviations. Should it not be possible to find groups of items meeting this less rigorous test of homogeneity, the series of situations would be judged definitely nonscalable by this technique, and other means of analysis would become necessary.

The example just cited suggests at least two other lines of development which are of considerable potential value. The first has to do with the crucial problem of techniques for analyzing *complex* opinions and actions. Unidimensional scales furnish a simple and excellent technique for isolating and treating opinions which lie along a single continuum. Analysis of the interrelations among scales and between scales and other indexes of behavior can throw considerable light upon the components of complex social actions. However, no matter how completely this can be done in any particular instance there remains the question of how to record and analyze the "clusters" of behavior which we can directly observe. Thus, as Merton has pointed out, attitude toward Negroes and education as a value complex is not likely to be revealed by combining separate scales of "attitude toward education" and "attitude toward the Negro." "Otherwise stated, the effort to attain a linear scale should not be permitted to divert all attention from the sociologically and psychologically relevant question of opinion-configurations." [57]

Insofar as future research may concern itself with field studies of whole communities—and this certainly seems a productive emphasis—there is need for the construction of indexes to measure fluctuations in intergroup relations on a community-wide basis. The city of Detroit has made a step in this direction in its use of an interracial "barometer" based on reports of specific incidents of friction. A more comprehensive and systematic battery of records would be valuable for research purposes. Such an inventory probably should include data on the numbers and types of acts of direct intergroup aggression, employment and income, the nature and extent of segregation, expressions of public opinion, and changes in formally organized groups. Given the necessary fact-finding organization, it would seem feasible to construct quantitative indexes of considerable usefulness for continuing community diagnosis.

Another promising line of development is the use of indirect or projective tests and generally nonmanifest methods of observation. Investigators of intergroup attitudes have recognized the possibility that in some situations the use of direct measuring instruments may itself change the phenomena being observed. Apparently such unintended effects are usually slight enough so that they can be ignored for most purposes. In comparisons of experimental and control groups any effects of the process of observation usually can be assumed to hold equally for the respective populations. The greatest danger is found when it is necessary to resort to test-retest procedures without a control group, especially if repeated observations are desired. In such situations it will be advantageous to use methods which do not reveal their purposes to respondents, or at least do not make it obvious that the situation is an experiment with intergroup problems. There is a possibility that the projective tests developed for personality study can be adapted for the investigation of intergroup attitudes. Explorations are being undertaken with the identification of photographs—an approach already used in personality diagnosis, as in the Szondi test. Recall of pictured or enacted scenes, and distortion in verbal relaying of descriptions are other possible methods which have been given preliminary trials. In work with children's groups

[57] Merton, op. cit., p. 19.

it appears feasible to use adaptations of the "guess-who" technique, the "show-me" tests, and various types of "doll-house" tests.

Finally, the evidence already available on the importance of the individual's social circle—the small intimate groups in which his most basic human relationships exist—in stabilizing his attitudes and behavior patterns shows the need for further development of methods for direct study of *group* behavior. It seems definitely established that the individual's social perception and total behavior are in part functions of his immediate social group, and that groups are more resistant to change than individuals apart from groups. The implications of such propositions for research have not been widely followed up. One immediate implication is the need for explicitly defining the group context within which observations are recorded. The works of Sherif, Lewin, and others have shown the technical feasibility of incorporating group factors into study designs.

A final word of caution is perhaps necessary after so much discussion of techniques and methods. *It is quite possible to emphasize research techniques to the point of sterility with regard to important substantive findings.* Too much time and talent can be diverted to the elaboration and refinement of devices for observation and measurement. Or, research workers may be too timid about attacking important problems merely because ideal tools are not available or ideal study designs not feasible at present. General verbal agreement is likely on the platitude that research techniques are simply means to the end of establishing principles of prediction and control—they are not goals in themselves. Verbal agreement is likewise easy to secure for the balancing proposition that if research is worth doing at all it warrants the best techniques available. However, in actual practice it is easy to fall into the spurious impasse between developing elaborate techniques which produce little of importance to social action, and hasty efforts to investigate significant problems by loose and inadequate methods. The most fruitful orientation at the present stage of research development in this field is probably the view that intensive work on improvement of research techniques should be an integral part of a many-sided attack on the problems of greatest scientific and practical importance. Techniques are tools for purposive action rather than materials for intellectual chess-playing; on the other hand, research does not necessarily lose its scientific status by reason of a focus on practical affairs.

SELECTED BIBLIOGRAPHY

1. ALEXANDER, FRANZ. Discussion of "Hostility and Fear in Social Life" by John Dollard, *Social Forces*, 17:27–29 (1938).
2. ALLPORT, GORDON W. "Catharsis and the Reduction of Prejudice," *Journal of Social Issues*, 1(3):3–10 (1945).
3. ————. Foreword in *A B C's of Scapegoating*. Chicago: Central Y.M.C.A. College, no date, c. 1943–44.
4. ————. *The Use of Personal Documents in Psychological Science*. Social Science Research Council Bulletin 49. New York, 1942.
5. ALLPORT, GORDON W. and BERNARD M. KRAMER. "Some Roots of Prejudice," *Journal of Psychology*, 22:9–39 (1946).
6. AMERICAN COUNCIL ON RACE RELATIONS. *Summary: Public Relations Workshop, September 27–8–9, 1946*. Chicago, 1947.
7. ANNIS, ALBERT D. "The Relative Effectiveness of Cartoons and Editorials as Propaganda Media" (abstract), *Psychological Bulletin*, 36:638 (1939).
8. APTHEKER, HERBERT. *The Negro People in America*. New York: International Publishers, 1946.
9. ASHER, R. and S. S. SARGENT. "Shifts in Attitude Caused by Cartoon Caricatures," *Journal of General Psychology*, 24:451–455 (1941).
10. BAKER, PAUL E. *Negro-White Adjustment*. New York: Association Press, 1934.
11. BALES, ROBERT F. "Social Therapy for a Social Disorder—Compulsive Drinking," *Journal of Social Issues*, 1(3):14–22 (1945).
12. BALLIN, MARIAN R. and PAUL R. FARNSWORTH, "A Graphic Rating Method for Determining the Scale Values of Statements in Measuring Social Attitudes," *Journal of Social Psychology*, 13:323–327 (1941).
13. BAYTON, JAMES A. "The Racial Stereotypes of Negro College Students," *Journal of Abnormal and Social Psychology*, 36:97–102 (1941).
14. BILLINGS, ELIZABETH L. "The Influence of a Social-Studies Experiment on Student Attitudes," *School and Society*, 56:557–560 (1942).
15. BLAKE, ROBERT and WAYNE DENNIS. "The Development of Stereotypes Concerning the Negro," *Journal of Abnormal and Social Psychology*, 38: 525–531 (1943).
16. BOGARDUS, EMORY S. "Measuring Social Distance," *Journal of Applied Sociology*, 9:299–308 (1925).
17. ————. "Race Friendliness and Social Distance," *Journal of Applied Sociology*, 11:272–287 (1927).
18. ————. "Sex Differences in Racial Attitudes," *Sociology and Social Research*, 12:279–285 (1928).
19. ————. "A Social Distance Scale," *Sociology and Social Research*, 17:265–271 (1933).
20. BOLTON, E. B. "Effect of Knowledge upon Attitude toward the Negro," *Journal of Social Psychology*, 6:68–90 (1935).
21. ————. "Measuring Specific Attitudes towards the Social Rights of the Negro," *Journal of Abnormal and Social Psychology*, 31:384–397 (1937).
22. BOWERS, RAYMOND V. "Discussion: An Analysis of the Problem of Validity," *American Sociological Review*, 1:69–74 (1936).

23. BOYNTON, PAUL L. and GEORGE D. MAYO. "A Comparison of Certain Attitudinal Responses of White and Negro High School Students," *Journal of
Negro Education,* 11:487–494 (1942).
24. BRAMELD, THEODORE. *Minority Problems in the Public Schools.* New York:
Harper & Brothers, 1946.
25. BRAMELD, THEODORE and ELEANOR FISH. "School Administration and Intercultural Relations," *The Annals,* 244:26–33 (1946).
26. BROOKS, LEE M. "Racial Distance as Affected by Education," *Sociology and
Social Research,* 21:128–133 (1936).
27. BROPHY, IRA N. "The Luxury of Anti-Negro Prejudice," *Public Opinion Quarterly,* 9:456–466 (1945–46).
28. BRYSON, LYMAN, LOUIS FINKELSTEIN and ROBERT M. MACIVER, eds. *Approaches
to National Unity: Fifth Symposium of the Conference on Science, Philosophy and Religion.* New York: Harper & Brothers, 1945.
29. BUROS, OSCAR K., ed. *Mental Measurements Yearbook.* New Brunswick:
Rutgers University Press, 1938.
30. CAMPBELL, DON W. and G. F. STOVER. "Teaching International-Mindedness
in the Social Studies," *Journal of Educational Sociology,* 7:244–248 (1933).
31. CANTRIL, HADLEY. *Gauging Public Opinion.* Princeton: Princeton University
Press, 1944.
32. CANTRIL, HADLEY and GORDON W. ALLPORT. *The Psychology of Radio.* New
York: Harper & Brothers, 1935.
33. CARLSON, H. B. "Attitudes of Undergraduate Students," *Journal of Social
Psychology,* 5:202–212 (1934).
34. CHASE, WILTON P. "Attitudes of North Carolina College Students (Women)
toward the Negro," *Journal of Social Psychology,* 12:367–378 (1940).
35. CHEN, WILLIAM K-C. "The Influence of Oral Propaganda Material upon
Students' Attitudes," *Archives of Psychology,* No. 150, 1933.
36. ———. "Retention of the Effect of Oral Propaganda," *Journal of Social
Psychology,* 7:479–483 (1936).
37. CHERRINGTON, BEN M. and L. W. MILLER. "Changes in Attitude as the Result
of a Lecture and of Reading Similar Materials," *Journal of Social Psychology,*
4:479–484 (1933).
38. CHICAGO COMMISSION ON RACE RELATIONS. *The Negro in Chicago.* University
of Chicago Press, 1922.
39. CHILD, IRVIN L. and LEONARD W. DOOB. "Factors Determining National
Stereotypes," *Journal of Social Psychology,* 17:203–219 (1943).
40. CLARK, KENNETH B. "Group Violence: A Preliminary Study of the Attitudinal
Pattern of Its Acceptance and Rejection: A Study of the 1943 Harlem
Riot," *Journal of Social Psychology,* 19:319–337 (1944).
41. CLARK, KENNETH B. and MAMIE K. CLARK. "Skin Color as a Factor in Racial
Identification of Negro Preschool Children," *Journal of Social Psychology,*
11:159–169 (1940).
42. CLINCHY, EVERETT R. "The Effort of Organized Religion," *The Annals,* 244:
128–136 (1946).
43. CLOSSON, E. E. "A Study of the Factor of Information in Race Prejudice."
Unpublished M.A. thesis, State University of Iowa, 1930.

44. COMMITTEE FOR RACIAL COOPERATION, BENJAMIN FRANKLIN HIGH SCHOOL. "Building Concepts of Racial Democracy" and "Appendix" in *Americans All: Studies in Intercultural Education*. Washington: National Education Association, 1942.

45. COOK, L. A. "An Experimental Sociographic Study of a Stratified Tenth Grade Class," *American Sociological Review*, 10:250–261 (1945).

46. COX, OLIVER C. "Race and Caste: A Distinction," *American Journal of Sociology*, 50:360–368 (1945).

47. CRISWELL, JOAN H. "Social Structure Revealed in a Sociometric Retest," *Sociometry*, 2:69–75 (1939).

48. ———. "A Sociometric Study of Race Cleavage in the Classroom," *Archives of Psychology*, No. 235, 1939.

49. DAVIDSON, H. A. "The Anatomy of Prejudice," *Common Ground*, 1(2):3–12 (1941).

50. DIGGINS, E. "A Statistical Study of National Prejudices." Unpublished M.A. thesis, Columbia University, 1927. Summarized in G. Murphy, L. B. Murphy and T. M. Newcomb, *Experimental Social Psychology*. New York: Harper & Brothers, 1931. Pp. 635–638.

51. *Directory of Agencies in Race Relations*. Chicago: Julius Rosenwald Fund, 1945.

52. DODD, STUART C. "A Social Distance Test in the Near East," *American Journal of Sociology*, 41:194–204 (1935).

53. DOLLARD, JOHN. *Caste and Class in a Southern Town*. New Haven: Yale University Press, 1937.

54. ———. *Criteria for the Life History*. New Haven: Yale University Press, 1935.

55. ———. "Hostility and Fear in Social Life," *Social Forces*, 17:15–26 (1938).

56. DOLLARD, JOHN and Others. *Frustration and Aggression*. New Haven: Yale University Press, 1939.

57. DOOB, LEONARD W. and ROBERT R. SEARS. "Factors Determining Substitute Behavior and the Overt Expression of Aggression," *Journal of Abnormal and Social Psychology*, 34:293–313 (1939).

58. DROBA, D. D. "Education and Negro Attitudes," *Sociology and Social Research*, 17:137–141 (1932).

59. EDWARDS, L. P. *The Natural History of Revolution*. Chicago: University of Chicago Press, 1927.

60. ELLIOTT, FRANK R. "Eye vs. Ear in Moulding Opinion," *Public Opinion Quarterly*, 1:83–87 (1936).

61. EWING, T. N. "A Study of Certain Factors Involved in Changes of Opinion," *Journal of Social Psychology*, 16:63–68 (1942).

62. FERGUSON, L. W. "The Requirements of an Adequate Attitude Scale," *Psychological Bulletin*, 36:665–673 (1939).

63. ———. "A Study of the Likert Technique of Attitude Scale Construction," *Journal of Social Psychology*, 13:51–57 (1941).

64. FINEBERG, S. A. *Overcoming Anti-Semitism*. New York: Harper & Brothers, 1933.

65. FORD, ROBERT N. "Scaling Experience by a Multiple-Response Technique: A Study of White-Negro Contacts," *American Sociological Review*, 6:9–23 (1941).

66. FREUD, S. *Group Psychology and the Analysis of the Ego.* London: The International Psycho-Analytical Press, 1922.

67. GARRISON, K. C. and J. S. BURCH. "A Study of Racial Attitudes of College Students," *Journal of Social Psychology*, 4:230–235 (1933).

68. GILES, H. H. and WILLIAM VAN TIL. "School and Community Projects," *The Annals*, 244:34–41 (1946).

69. GLICKSBERG, CHARLES I. "Intercultural Education: Utopia or Reality," *Common Ground*, 6(4):61–68 (1946).

70. GOTTSCHALK, LOUIS, CLYDE KLUCKHOHN and ROBERT ANGELL. *The Use of Personal Documents in History, Anthropology, and Sociology.* Social Science Research Council Bulletin 53. New York, 1945.

71. GRAEBER, ISACQUE and STEUART H. BRITT, eds. *Jews in a Gentile World.* New York: The Macmillan Company, 1942.

72. GREEN, GEORGE H. "Have Children a National Bias?" *Discovery*, 13:44–46 (1932).

73. GREENWOOD, ERNEST. *Experimental Sociology: A Study in Method.* New York: Kings Crown Press, 1945.

74. GRICE, H. H. and H. H. REMMERS. *A Scale for Measuring Attitudes toward Races and Nationalities.* Lafayette: Purdue Research Foundation, Purdue University, 1934.

75. GROSSER, G. H. and S. J. KORCHIN. "Some Theoretical Aspects of Group Prejudice and Conflict." Mimeographed paper, Harvard University Seminar on Group Prejudice and Conflict, fall term, 1944–45.

76. GUILFORD, J. P. "Racial Preferences of a Thousand American University Students," *Journal of Social Psychology*, 2:179–204 (1931).

77. GUTTMAN, LOUIS. "A Basis for Scaling Qualitative Data," *American Sociological Review*, 9:139–150 (1944).

78. HAAG, H. L. "Study of Racial Attitudes of High School and University Students." Unpublished M.A. thesis, University of Michigan, 1930. Cited in Murphy, Murphy and Newcomb, *op. cit.* 1937 edition. Pp. 982–983.

79. HAAS, F. J. and G. J. FLEMING. "Personnel Practices and Wartime Changes," *The Annals*, 244:48–56 (1946).

80. HARLAN, HOWARD H. "Some Factors Affecting Attitude toward Jews," *American Sociological Review*, 7:816–827 (1942).

81. HARRIS, A. J., H. H. REMMERS and C. E. ELLISON. "The Relation between Liberal and Conservative Attitudes in College Students, and Other Factors," *Journal of Social Psychology*, 3:320–335 (1932).

82. HARTLEY, E. L. and A. MINTZ. "A Technique for the Study of the Dynamics of the Racial Saturation Point," *Sociometry*, 9:14–20 (1946).

83. HARTMANN, G. W. "A Field Experiment on the Comparative Effectiveness of 'Emotional' and 'Rational' Political Leaflets in Determining Election Results," *Journal of Abnormal and Social Psychology*, 31:99–114 (1936).

84. HAYNES, G. E. "Public Approbation as a Means of Changing Interracial Attitudes and Customs," *Social Forces*, 24:105–110 (1945).

85. HEINRICH, J. C. *The Psychology of a Suppressed People.* London: George Allen & Unwin, 1937.
86. HILDRETH, GERTRUDE H. *A Bibliography of Mental Tests and Rating Scales.* 2nd edition. New York: The Psychological Corporation, 1939.
87. HILLER, E. T. *The Strike.* Chicago: University of Chicago Press, 1928.
88. HINCKLEY, E. D. "The Influence of Individual Opinion on Construction of an Attitude Scale," *Journal of Social Psychology,* 3:283–295 (1932).
89. HORNEY, KAREN. *The Neurotic Personality of Our Time.* New York: W. W. Norton and Co., 1937.
90. HOROWITZ, E. L. "The Development of Attitude Toward the Negro," *Archives of Psychology,* No. 194, 1936.
91. HOROWITZ, E. L. and R. E. HOROWITZ. "Development of Social Attitudes in Children," *Sociometry,* 1:301–338 (1938).
92. HUNTER, C. W. "A Comparative Study of the Relationships Existing between the White and Negro Race in the State of North Carolina and the City of New York." Unpublished M.A. thesis, Columbia University, 1927. Cited in Murphy, Murphy and Newcomb, *op. cit.* 1937 edition. Pp. 927–928.
93. ICHHEISER, GUSTAV. "Fear of Violence and Fear of Fraud." *Sociometry,* 7:376–383 (1944).
94. ————. "The Jews and Anti-Semitism," *Sociometry,* 9:92–108 (1946).
95. "Jews in America," *Fortune,* 13(2):79–85, 128–144 (1936).
96. JOHNSON, CHARLES S. "Measurement of Racial Attitudes," *American Sociological Society Publications,* 25(2):150–153 (1931).
97. ————. "National Organizations in the Field of Race Relations," *The Annals,* 244:117–127 (1946).
98. ————. *Patterns of Negro Segregation.* New York: Harper & Brothers, 1943.
99. ————. "Racial Attitudes of College Students," *American Sociological Society Publications,* 28(2):24–31 (1934).
100. JONES, VERNON. "Attitudes of College Students Toward War, Race, and Religion, and the Changes in Such Attitudes During Four Years in College" (abstract), *Psychological Bulletin,* 33:731–732 (1936).
101. KATZ, DANIEL and F. H. ALLPORT. *Students' Attitudes.* Syracuse: Craftsman Press, 1931.
102. KATZ, DANIEL and K. BRALY. "Racial Stereotypes of One Hundred College Students," *Journal of Abnormal and Social Psychology,* 28:280–290 (1933).
103. KLINEBERG, OTTO, ed. *Characteristics of the American Negro.* New York: Harper & Brothers, 1944.
104. KLUCKHOHN, CLYDE. "Group Tensions: Analysis of a Case History," in Bryson, Finkelstein and MacIver, *op. cit.* Pp. 222–241.
105. ————. "Navajo Witchcraft," *Harvard University, Papers of the Peabody Museum,* Vol. 22, No. 2 (1944).
106. KLUCKHOHN, FLORENCE. "The Participant-Observer Technique in Small Communities," *American Journal of Sociology,* 46:331–343 (1940).
107. KNOWER, FRANKLIN H. "Experimental Studies of Changes in Attitude: I. A Study of the Effect of Oral Argument on Changes of Attitude," *Journal of Social Psychology,* 6:315–345 (1935); ". . . II. A Study of the Effect of Printed Argument on Changes in Attitude," *Journal of Abnormal and*

Social Psychology, 30:522–532 (1936); ". . . III. Some Incidence of Attitude Changes," *Journal of Applied Psychology,* 20:114–127 (1936).

108. KOENIG, S. "Ethnic Factors in the Economic Life of Urban Connecticut," *American Sociological Review,* 8:193–197 (1943).

109. KULP, DANIEL H., II. "The Form of Statements in Attitude Tests," *Sociology and Social Research,* 18:18–25 (1933).

110. ————. "Prestige, as Measured by Single-Experience Changes and Their Permanency," *Journal of Educational Research,* 27:663–672 (1934).

111. LAPIERE, R. T. "Attitudes vs. Actions," *Social Forces,* 13:230–237 (1934).

112. ————. "Race Prejudice: France and England," *Social Forces,* 7:102–111 (1928).

113. LASKER, BRUNO. *Race Attitudes in Children.* New York: Henry Holt and Company, 1929.

114. LAZARSFELD, P. F. "The Controversy over Detailed Interviews—An Offer for Negotiation," *Public Opinion Quarterly,* 8:38–60 (1944).

115. LETT, H. A. "Techniques for Achieving Interracial Cooperation," *Proceedings of the Institute on Race Relations and Community Organization, June, 1945.* University of Chicago and American Council on Race Relations.

116. LEVINE, J. M. and G. MURPHY. "The Learning and Forgetting of Controversial Materials," *Journal of Abnormal and Social Psychology,* 38:507–517 (1943).

117. LEVINSON, D. J. and R. N. SANFORD. "A Scale for the Measurement of Anti-Semitism," *Journal of Psychology,* 17:339–370 (1944).

118. LEWIN, KURT. "Forces behind Food Habits and Methods of Change," *National Research Council Bulletin* No. 108, pp. 35–65 (1943).

119. ————. "Psycho-Sociological Problems of a Minority Group," *Character and Personality,* 3:175–187 (1935).

120. ————. "Research on Minority Problems," *Technology Review,* 48:163–164, 182–190 (1946).

121. LEWIN, KURT and PAUL GRABBE. "Conduct, Knowledge, and Acceptance of New Values," *Journal of Social Issues,* 1(3):53–64 (1945).

122. LEWIN, KURT, RONALD LIPPITT and RALPH K. WHITE. "Patterns of Aggressive Behavior in Experimentally Created 'Social Climates,'" *Journal of Social Psychology,* 10:271–299 (1939).

123. LIKERT, RENSIS. "A Technique for the Measurement of Attitudes," *Archives of Psychology,* No. 140, 1932.

124. LIKERT, RENSIS, SYDNEY ROSLOW and GARDNER MURPHY. "A Simple and Reliable Method of Scoring the Thurstone Attitude Scales," *Journal of Social Psychology,* 5:228–238 (1934).

125. LINK, H. C. "An Experiment in Depth Interviewing on the Issue of Internationalism vs. Isolationism," *Public Opinion Quarterly,* 7:267–279 (1943).

126. LIPPITT, RONALD and MARIAN RADKE. "New Trends in the Investigation of Prejudice," *The Annals,* 244:167–176 (1946).

127. LIVERIGHT, A. A. "The Community and Race Relations," *The Annals,* 244:106–116 (1946).

128. LOEBLOWITZ-LENNARD, HENRY and FRANK RIESSMAN, JR. "A Preliminary Report on a Social Perception Test: A New Approach to Attitude Research," *Social Forces,* 24:423–427 (1946).

129. Lorge, Irving. "Prestige, Suggestion and Attitudes" (abstract), *Psychological Bulletin*, 32:750 (1935).

130. Low, A. Ritchie. "Invitation to Vermont," *Common Ground*, 6(4):44–52 (1946).

131. MacCrone, I. D. *Race Attitudes in South Africa.* London: Oxford University Press, 1937.

132. Manske, A. J. "The Reflection of Teachers' Attitudes in the Attitudes of Their Pupils." Unpublished Ph.D. thesis, Teachers College, Columbia University, 1935. Reported in Murphy, Murphy and Newcomb, *op. cit.* 1937 edition. Pp. 950–951.

133. Marcson, Simon. "The Control of Ethnic Conflict," *Social Forces*, 24:161–165 (1945).

134. Marks, Eli S. "Standardization of a Race Attitude Test for Negro Youth," *Journal of Social Psychology*, 18:245–278 (1943).

135. Marple, Clare H. "The Comparative Susceptibility of Three Age Levels to the Suggestion of Group versus Expert Opinion," *Journal of Social Psychology*, 4:176–184 (1933).

136. Maslow, A. H. "Deprivation, Threat, and Frustration," *Psychological Review*, 48:364–367 (1941).

137. McNemar, Quinn. "Opinion-Attitude Methodology," *Psychological Bulletin*, 43:289–374 (1946).

138. McWilliams, Carey. *Prejudice: Japanese-Americans: Symbol of Racial Intolerance.* Boston: Little, Brown and Company, 1944.

139. ———. "Race Discrimination and the Law," *Science & Society*, 9:1–22 (1945).

140. Meltzer, H. "The Development of Children's Nationality Preferences, Concepts, and Attitudes," *Journal of Psychology*, 11:343–358 (1941).

141. ———. "Group Differences in Nationality and Race Preferences of Children," *Sociometry*, 2:86–105 (1939).

142. ———. "Hostility and Tolerance in Children's Nationality and Race Attitudes," *American Journal of Orthopsychiatry*, 11:662–675 (1941).

143. Merton, Robert K. "Fact and Factitiousness in Ethnic Opinionnaires," *American Sociological Review*, 5:13–28 (1940).

144. Merton, Robert K. and Patricia L. Kendall. "The Focused Interview," *American Journal of Sociology*, 51:541–557 (1946).

145. Miller, H. A. *Races, Nations, and Classes.* Philadelphia: J. B. Lippincott Company, 1924.

146. Minard, Ralph D. "Race Attitudes of Iowa Children," *University of Iowa Studies in Character.* Vol. 4, No. 2 (1931).

147. Mintz, A. and E. L. Horowitz. "Differential Test Responses to Differently Qualified Members of Ethnic Groups." Unpublished paper. Cited by Horowitz in Klineberg, *op. cit.* P. 148.

148. Monjar, Elsie. "Racial Distance Reactions," *Sociology and Social Research*, 21:559–564 (1937).

149. Moreno, J. L. *Who Shall Survive?* Washington: Nervous and Mental Disease Publishing Co., 1934.

150. Morgan, John J. B. "Attitudes of Students toward the Japanese," *Journal of Social Psychology*, 21:219–227 (1945).

151. MURPHY, GARDNER and RENSIS LIKERT. *Public Opinion and the Individual.* New York: Harper & Brothers, 1938.

152. MURPHY, GARDNER, LOIS B. MURPHY and THEODORE M. NEWCOMB. *Experimental Social Psychology.* New York: Harper & Brothers, 1931; 1937.

153. MURRAY, H. A. and Others. *Explorations in Personality.* New York: Oxford University Press, 1938.

154. MYRDAL, GUNNAR, with the assistance of RICHARD STERNER and ARNOLD ROSE. *An American Dilemma.* New York: Harper & Brothers, 1944.

155. NETTLER, GWYNNE. "The Relationship Between Attitude and Information Concerning the Japanese in America," *American Sociological Review,* 11:177–191 (1946).

156. NETTLER, GWYNNE and ELIZABETH H. GOLDING. "The Measurement of Attitudes toward the Japanese in America," *American Journal of Sociology,* 52:31–39 (1946).

157. PACE, C. ROBERT. "A Situations Test to Measure Social-Political-Economic Attitudes," *Journal of Social Psychology,* 10:331–344 (1939).

158. PARSONS, TALCOTT. "Propaganda and Social Control," *Psychiatry,* 5:551–572 (1942).

159. ———. "Racial and Religious Differences as Factors in Group Tensions," in Bryson, Finkelstein and MacIver, *op. cit.* Pp. 182–199.

160. ———. "The Sociology of Modern Anti-Semitism," in Graeber and Britt, *op. cit.* Pp. 101–122.

161. PETERSON, RUTH C. and L. L. THURSTONE. *Motion Pictures and the Social Attitudes of Children.* New York: The Macmillan Company, 1933.

162. PETTEE, GEORGE S. *The Process of Revolution.* Studies in Systematic Political Science and Comparative Government, Vol. 5. New York: Harper & Brothers, 1938.

163. PITTMAN, R. H. "Building an Interracial Church," *Sociology and Social Research,* 29:297–303 (1945).

164. PORTERFIELD, AUSTIN L. "Education and Race Attitudes," *Sociology and Social Research,* 21:538–543 (1937).

165. POWDERMAKER, HORTENSE. "The Channeling of Negro Aggression by the Cultural Process," *American Journal of Sociology,* 48:750–758 (1943).

166. ———. *Probing Our Prejudices.* New York: Harper & Brothers, 1944.

167. Progressive Education Association, Evaluation in the Eight Year Study. *Scales of Belief.* Chicago: University of Chicago Press, 1939.

168. PROSHANSKY, H. M. "A Projective Method for the Study of Attitudes," *Journal of Abnormal and Social Psychology,* 38:393–395 (1943).

169. RAPER, ARTHUR F. *The Tragedy of Lynching.* Chapel Hill: University of North Carolina Press, 1933.

170. RECKLESS, WALTER C. and HAROLD L. BRINGEN. "Racial Attitudes and Information About the Negro," *Journal of Negro Education,* 2:128–138 (1933).

171. REMMERS, H. H. "Propaganda in the Schools—Do the Effects Last?" *Public Opinion Quarterly,* 2:197–210 (1938).

172. REUTER, E. B. "Racial Theory," *American Journal of Sociology,* 50:452–461 (1945).

173. RICH, BENNETT M. *The Presidents and Civil Disorder.* Washington: The Brookings Institution, 1941.

174. ROBINSON, DUANE and SYLVIA ROHDE. "A Public Opinion Study of Anti-Semitism in New York City," *American Sociological Review,* 10:511–515 (1945).

175. ————. "Two Experiments with an Anti-Semitism Poll," *Journal of Abnormal and Social Psychology,* 41:136–144 (1946).

176. ROETHLISBERGER, F. J. *Management and Morale.* Cambridge: Harvard University Press, 1941.

177. ROGERS, CARL R. *Counseling and Psychotherapy.* Boston: Houghton Mifflin Company, 1942.

178. ————. "The Nondirective Method as a Technique for Social Research," *American Journal of Sociology,* 50:279–283 (1945).

179. ROSANDER, A. C. "An Attitude Scale Based upon Behavior Situations," *Journal of Social Psychology,* 8:3–15 (1937).

180. ROSE, ARNOLD M. *Studies in Reduction of Prejudice.* Chicago: American Council on Race Relations, 1947. Mimeographed.

181. RUBIN, ABRAHAM and GEORGE J. SEGAL. "An Industrial Experiment," *The Annals,* 244:57–64 (1946).

182. RUNDQUIST, E. A. and R. F. SLETTO. *Personality in the Depression.* Minneapolis: University of Minnesota Press, 1936.

183. SAADI, MITCHEL and PAUL R. FARNSWORTH. "The Degrees of Acceptance of Dogmatic Statements and Preferences for Their Supposed Makers," *Journal of Abnormal and Social Psychology,* 29:143–150 (1934).

184. SAMELSON, BABETTE. "Does Education Diminish Prejudice?" *Journal of Social Issues,* 1(3):11–13 (1945).

185. ————. "Mrs. Jones's Ethnic Attitudes: A Ballot Analysis," *Journal of Abnormal and Social Psychology,* 40:205–214 (1945).

186. SAPPENFIELD, BERT R. "The Responses of Catholic, Protestant, and Jewish Students to the Menace Checklist," *Journal of Social Psychology,* 20:295–299 (1944).

187. SCHLORFF, P. W. "An Experiment in the Measurement and Modification of Racial Attitudes in School Children." Unpublished Ph.D. thesis, New York University, 1930. Reported in F. Tredwell Smith, *An Experiment in Modifying Attitudes toward the Negro,* New York: Teachers College, Columbia University, 1943. Pp. 15–16.

188. SEASHORE, R. H. and K. A. HEVNER. "A Time-Saving Device for the Construction of Attitude Scales," *Journal of Social Psychology,* 4:366–372 (1933).

189. SHEEHY, MAURICE S. and National Attitudes Committee. *National Attitudes in Children.* Catholic Association for International Peace, Pamphlet No. 10. Washington, 1932.

190. SHERIF, MUZAFER. *The Psychology of Social Norms.* New York: Harper & Brothers, 1936.

191. SIMS, V. M. and J. R. PATRICK. "Attitude toward the Negro of Northern and Southern College Students," *Journal of Social Psychology,* 7:192–204 (1936).

192. SLETTO, RAYMOND F. *Construction of Personality Scales by the Criterion of Internal Consistency.* Minneapolis: The Sociological Press, 1937.

193. SMITH, F. TREDWELL. *An Experiment in Modifying Attitudes toward the Negro,* New York: Teachers College, Columbia University, 1943.

194. SMITH, MAPHEUS. "A Study of Change of Attitudes toward the Negro," *Journal of Negro Education,* 8:64–70 (1939); "A Second Report on Changes in Attitudes toward the Negro," *School and Society,* 57:388–392 (1943).

195. STRONG, DONALD S. *Organized Anti-Semitism in the United States.* Washington: American Council on Public Affairs, 1941.

196. STROTHER, CHARLES R. "Methods of Modifying Behavior," *Journal of Social Issues,* 1(3):46–52 (1945).

197. TABA, HILDA and WILLIAM VAN TIL, eds. *Democratic Human Relations.* National Council for the Social Studies, Yearbook. Washington, 1946.

198. THOMAS, JULIUS A. "War-Time Changes in the Occupational Status of Negro Workers," *Occupations,* 23:402–405 (1945).

199. THURSTONE, L. L. "Attitudes Can Be Measured," *American Journal of Sociology,* 33:529–554 (1928).

200. ————. "An Experimental Study of Nationality Preferences," *Journal of General Psychology,* 1:405–425 (1928).

201. THURSTONE, L. L. and E. J. CHAVE. *The Measurement of Attitude.* Chicago: University of Chicago Press, 1929.

202. TURBEVILLE, GUS and ROY E. HYDE. "A Selected Sample of Attitudes of Louisiana State University Students toward the Negro: A Study in Public Opinion," *Social Forces,* 24:447–450 (1946).

203. VETTER, G. B. "The Measurement of Social and Political Attitudes and the Related Personality Factors," *Journal of Abnormal and Social Psychology,* 25:149–189 (1930).

204. VICKERY, W. E. and S. G. COLE. *Intercultural Education in American Schools.* New York: Harper & Brothers, 1943.

205. WANG, CHARLES K. A. "Suggested Criteria for Writing Attitude Statements," *Journal of Social Psychology,* 3:367–373 (1932).

206. WANGER, R. "High School Study of the Negro and His Problems," *High School Teacher,* 8:104–106 (1932).

207. WATSON, GOODWIN. *Action for Unity.* New York: Harper & Brothers, 1946.

208. ————. *Opinions on Race Relations.* New York: Association Press, 1929.

209. ————. "Orient and Occident: An Opinion Study," *Religious Education,* 24:322–328 (1929).

210. ————. "The Problem of Evaluation," *The Annals,* 244:177–182 (1946).

211. WEAVER, ROBERT C. "Housing in a Democracy," *The Annals,* 244:95–105 (1946).

212. WHISLER, LAURENCE. "Changes in Attitudes towards Social Issues Accompanying a One-Year Freshman Social Science Course," *Journal of Psychology,* 10:387–396 (1940).

213. WILKE, WALTER H. "An Experimental Comparison of the Speech, the Radio, and the Printed Page as Propaganda Devices," *Archives of Psychology,* No. 169, 1934.

214. WOLF, E. P., A. D. LOVING and D. C. MARSH. "Negro-Jewish Relationships," *Wayne University Studies in Intergroup Conflicts in Detroit.* Detroit: Wayne University Press, 1944.

215. WRIGHTSTONE, J. W. *Scale of Civic Beliefs.* Chicago: World Book Company, 1939.

216. YOUNG, DONALD. *American Minority Peoples.* New York: Harper & Brothers, 1932.

217. ————. *Research Memorandum on Minority Peoples in the Depression.* Social Science Research Council Bulletin 31. New York, 1937.

218. ————. "Some Effects of a Course in American Race Problems on the Race Prejudice of 450 Undergraduates at the University of Pennsylvania," *Journal of Abnormal and Social Psychology,* 22:235–242 (1927).

219. YOUNG, ERLE F. "The Relation of Lynching to the Size of Political Areas," *Sociology and Social Research,* 12:348–353 (1928).

220. YOUNG, KIMBALL. *Social Psychology.* New York: F. S. Crofts and Company, 1935.

221. ZELIGS, ROSE. "Tracing Racial Attitudes through Adolescence," *Sociology and Social Research,* 23:45–54 (1938).

222. ZELIGS, ROSE and GORDON HENDRICKSON. "Racial Attitudes of Two Hundred Sixth-Grade Children," *Sociology and Social Research,* 18:26–36 (1933).

223. ZILBOORG, GREGORY. "Paternalistic Aggression and Individual Freedom in the Present Crisis," *American Journal of Orthopsychiatry,* 11:638–642 (1941).

INDEX OF SUBJECTS

Observation, as research technique, 116, 119

Opinion studies, *see* Attitudes

Organizations, in field of race relations: assumptions of programs of, 10–16; numbers and programs, 7

Personalization, effect of, in reducing hostility, 66

Police, training of, 87

Political means of reducing conflict, 21; *see also* Law

Prejudice: concept and types of, 36–39, 42; economic determinants of, 13–14; effects of religious training on, 68; formation in children, 81–82; as function of ignorance, 13; relation to contact, 38, 40, 71; relation to group self-consciousness, 63; relation to individual values, 62; relation to personality, 80; relation to psychological needs, 14; *see also* Negro, prejudice against; Anti-Semitism

Prestige symbols: experimental study of effectiveness of, 32; use of, 19

Projective techniques, 123–124

Proof, adequacy of, 25

Propaganda: class, sectional reaction to, 89; classified by media, 20; effectiveness of, 31–32, 67; *see also* Education

Psychotherapy, 24

Public Affairs Committee, 21

Publicity, effects of, on tensions, 15, 16

Punishment, relation to aggression, 53

Quantitative methods, classification of studies using, 28–30

Questionnaires, 121–122

Race riots, 4, 43–44, 60

Racial groups, defined, 42

Recreation, 100–102

Religion: as factor in prejudice, 68; research into effects of, 87–88; as shared value, 42, 55

Research: contribution to action, 9–10; contribution to educational programs, 83–84; deficiencies of, 33, 34; inadequacies of early orientation of, 47;

lack of, in action programs, 8, 33; practical values of, 106; resistance to, 9; techniques of, 24–25, 80, 116–124

Role-taking, 72, 87

Rumor, 68

Sampling theory, 116–117

Segregation, 74; *see also* Discrimination

Self-written documents, 123

Sociometric technique, 93, 120

Southern Regional Council, 12, 24

Statistical techniques, 117

Teaching, testing effects of, 86–88

Techniques: for controlling behavior, 10–11, 17–19, 63, 72–73, 133; *see also* Projective techniques; Research, techniques of

Tennessee Valley Authority, 81

Tension level of society, 4, 55

Textbooks, content analysis of, 90

Transference of behavior, 16

Unidimensional scales, advantages of, 130–132

Unionization, 22, 95, 102–104

United States Army, 128

United States War Department, 114n, 120n, 128n

Urban League, 12

Validity, 114, 130

Values: American system of, 2, 3, 5, 60; direct reorientation of, 66–68; divisive or shared, 55–56; as factor in focusing hostility, 54; as factor in reducing conflict, 75; as factor in social tension, 55; means of changing, 14; real intergroup differences in, 82

"Vicious circle," 45

Violence: in conflict situation, 74; prevalence of, 1, 4

Visibility, relation to focus of hostility, 54

Yale University, 80

Young Men's Christian Association, 23

Young Women's Christian Association, 23

INDEX OF NAMES